W9-ATT-923

Haunted
Maryland

Ghosts and Strange Phenomena
of the Old Line State

Ed Okonowicz

Illustrations by Heather Adel Wiggins

STACKPOLE
BOOKS

0 11557 03409 7

Copyright © 2007 by Edward M. Okonowicz Jr.

Published by
STACKPOLE BOOKS
5067 Ritter Road
Mechanicsburg, PA 17055
www.stackpolebooks.com

All rights reserved, including the right to reproduce this book or portions thereof in any form or by any means, electronic or mechanical, including photocopying, recording, or by any information storage and retrieval system, without permission in writing from the publisher. All inquiries should be addressed to Stackpole Books.

Printed in the United States of America

10 9 8 7 6 5 4 3 2 1

FIRST EDITION

Cover design by Caroline Stover

Library of Congress Cataloging-in-Publication Data

Okonowicz, E, 1947–
    Haunted Maryland : ghosts and strange phenomena of the Old Line State. / Ed Okonowicz.
        p.   cm.
    Includes bibliographical references.
    ISBN-13: 978-0-8117-3409-7 (pbk.)
    ISBN-10: 0-8117-3409-9 (pbk.)
    1. Ghosts—Maryland. 2. Haunted places—Maryland. 3. Parapsychology—Maryland. I. Title.
BF1472.U6O553   2007
133.109752—dc22

                                        2006102022

Contents

Contents

Introduction

PEOPLE OFTEN ASK ME IF I BELIEVE IN GHOSTS. MY INITIAL RESPONSE IS an immediate, automatic, and truthful "Yes!" But I quickly add that my "Yes" is qualified by the following: "Yes! Because I believe there are some rather strange things happening out there." These unusual, paranormal, mysterious, and unexplainable events might be caused by ghosts, spirits, demons, aliens, trolls, snallygasters, angels, or a combination of the yet-to-be-discovered creatures waiting for their own special identifying word to be listed in a future dictionary.

After all, since biblical times and through all the centuries of recorded history, references have been made regarding events, sightings, and circumstances generally referred to as "unexplained." I'll admit that some eerie happenings are simply coincidences, incorrectly identified incidents, products of overactive and overeager imaginations, and even downright lies told to gain attention. But not all.

There *are* things that go bump in the night. There *are* occurrences that highly credentialed scientists cannot explain. There *are* government cover-ups. There *are* certain people who have a psychic "gift" or a "sixth sense." And I truly believe that some people have had near-death experiences, have been visited by aliens, or have been contacted by messengers or departed loved ones from the other side.

This is my seventeenth book about the paranormal. It features incidents and unusual happenings throughout the entire state of Maryland; however, please keep in mind that not every story, legend, ghost tale, or unusual event is included between these covers. This is only an overview of Maryland's numerous ghost tales. A comprehensive collection would fill many volumes, and there would still be items overlooked—plus additional incidents that would have occurred while the latest "complete" collection was being printed and bound.

And, for sure, readers will remark that some of their local "favorites" have been omitted. Without argument, I agree. The stories in this book are the best I could find—within the publisher's deadline—after searching old records, interviewing folks, and tracking down leads that went somewhere (and a fair number that went nowhere). So if your special haunted site is omitted, feel free to contact me, and I will do my best to include it in my future volumes.

While conducting my research, I came across an interesting article, "On the Hunt for Haunts," published in the *Washington Post* on October 28, 1993. Reporter David Montgomery made two noteworthy observations: "The State of Maryland is the single largest local owner of haunted real estate" and "the greatest threat to ghosts and demons is neither ghostbusters nor exorcists: it is suburban sprawl, which has killed at least two local ghost stories by turning once-lonely, haunted roads into safe and sterile subdivisions."

In the years since Montgomery's article appeared, too many rural forested acres, spooky lanes, abandoned buildings, and historic sites have been replaced with cookie-cutter developments, modern offices, strip malls, and wider roads. With this acceptance of progress and convenience, we trade away more links with our mysterious past. During this ghost-searching and ghost-writing adventure, I have learned that history shares a solid, ever-present link with folklore and legend—and that there is an ageless human need for a good scary story.

That's what this process is all about: finding the unusual tale and delivering it to you, the reader. Your decision to buy this book probably was based on the title and cover. Now, as you move into the written work, I hope you find the stories to be worth your time and money. I hope that within these pages, along with some fascinating tales and legends, you'll discover the wealth of significant history that occurred in the Old Line State and how important those events were to the founding, development, and decision making in our country.

These stories have grown out of experiences that occurred when settlers arrived in 1634 on Maryland's uncharted shores, when young men fought in several wars to defend and establish our nation's freedom, and when families pulled up stakes and followed their dreams, heading west to explore uncharted lands.

While Maryland is not the nation's largest state, many major players in America's founding and growth lived and visited here. Three noted examples include Francis Scott Key, who wrote the words to our national anthem during the bombardment of Fort McHenry; author Edgar Allan Poe, who created the horror genre in fiction; and John Wilkes Booth, a native son of Maryland, who became America's most infamous assassin.

Because of the colony's central location—between New York and Philadelphia to the north and Washington and Richmond to the south—explorers, murderers, and politicians, as well as businessmen, slave traders, soldiers, and Indians, passed along Maryland's waterways and early highways. As a result, Maryland's past is filled with adventures of the famous, the infamous, and the forgotten that are waiting to be shared. These are some of the stories that I think are worth your time.

Happy reading.

Eastern Shore

EVERY STATE HAS NAMES FOR ITS REGIONS, AND IN MARYLAND THE MOST famous is the Eastern Shore. For centuries, these nine counties east of the Chesapeake Bay—Cecil, Kent, Queen Anne's, Talbot, Caroline, Dorchester, Somerset, Wicomico, and Worcester—have maintained their unique regional culture, and on several occasions, this distinctively independent region (which makes up the largest section of this book) has even considered seceding from the rest of the state. In fact, this significant portion of Maryland—along with the state of Delaware and two counties of the eastern shore of Virginia—makes up a fourteen-county region known as the Delmarva Peninsula.

With hundreds of waterways, streams, and hidden coves, the names of pirates, watermen, sea monsters, and swamp ghosts are an accepted and natural part of Eastern Shore residents' vocabulary.

Among the area legends in this section, you'll meet a trio of horrifying female spirits—namely, Screaming Polly, Patty Cannon, and Bigg Lizz. Each has her own chilling tale to share, and each is believed to still roam the guts and coves of Maryland's Eastern Shore.

Bleeding Stone of White House Farm

There's a single rock, resting on a knoll behind a farmhouse. Occasionally, strangers stop along MD Route 213, a well-traveled Kent

County roadway. They want to sneak a peek or take a picture of "the bleeding stone."

Mention the rock to the locals and they'll tell you "it bleeds." Some will add they saw blood seeping out from the rock. Others admit that they've only heard the story but never actually saw anything unusual firsthand. But whether they saw the blood flow or not, the rock reminds visitors of the tale of a restless young girl with hopes and dreams, who died hundreds of years ago.

Most likely, the fatal accident took place during early morning when the young indentured-servant girl rode off, intending to escape with her lover from the daily boredom associated with her chores and life at White House Farm. But happily ever after was not to be, for within minutes after leaving the farmhouse—which still stands south of Kennedyville, about five miles north of Chestertown—her exciting new life did not begin. Instead, her miserable former one ended.

The most universal version of the legend claims the young girl's horse fell in the dark field. As her body left the saddle and slid across the damp surface, her head smashed against a rock—a solitary stone that should have been easier to avoid than to find—and there she bled to death. No one knows the young woman's name or that of her lover, who had lured her away with promises of romance and independence, but her story remains firmly entrenched in Eastern Shore folklore

Originally called the Ridgely Estate, the oldest section of the home was built by the Isaac Perkins family in the early eighteenth century. The date "1721" is visible on the outside of one end of the long, white farmhouse.

Colonel Isaac Perkins was described as a "Flaming Patriot." Records indicate that the mill on his property supplied flour to Washington's army while it was waiting out the winter at Valley Forge, Pennsylvania. According to additional documents in the state of Maryland archives, General Washington stopped at White House Farm occasionally while he was traveling on the old road that is now MD Route 213. In fact, some suggest that the nation's first president may well be one of the ghosts who sometimes visits the house.

During an interview in 1995 for the book *Opening the Door,* long-time owner Kathryn Pinder shared her experiences in White House Farm, which she and her late husband Arthur had bought in

1944. The legend of the "bleeding stone" was so well known, Mrs. Pinder said, that when the state highway department changed the course of Route 213 several years ago—widening it and placing the highway in the path of where the stone was situated—the stone was moved from its original site and placed at the top of the hill near the farmhouse.

"The bloodstained stone is in the rear yard," Mrs. Pinder said. "According to legend, a young girl eloping on horseback was thrown and killed when her head hit the large rock. It can be painted or whitewashed," she added, "but the bloodstain will eventually reappear."

People stop by to see "the stone" often, she said. In 1992, her home was entered on the National Register of Historic Places, and its history and ghosts have been featured in books, in newspaper articles, and on Baltimore television programs.

Not surprisingly, such an old house has its share of bumps and thuds in the night, and the former owner told about a few of her own encounters. Before moving into the French Colonial–style farmhouse, the Pinders were painting the kitchen and heard footsteps coming from one of the rooms upstairs. She also said they had heard sounds during their years in the home and one time saw an apparition of a lady wearing a blue nightgown. But there were other mysterious tales related to the home that attracted the owner's attention.

Perhaps the most interesting ghost associated with White House Farm is the spirit of Mary Perkins Stuart, who inherited the family farm in 1768 upon the death of her father when she was but a small child. She died at age thirty-nine, on January 8, 1803.

Her grave rests beside that of her father, Thomas Perkins, in the family plot, located across the two-lane road and about a quarter mile beyond the fields from the historic farmhouse. The two leaning grave markers are worn, indicating their futile battle to hold back the effects of the elements. The overgrowth of the advancing wood line and downed trees make the gravesites difficult to find.

On Mary's gravestone, a long epitaph that reaches from tip to base describes her as ". . . pious, friendly and humane, amiable in disposition and as a wife and mother most affectionate, soothing and endearing . . . perfectly sensible and resigned, the last breathings of her soul were 'come Lord, let us come quickly.' . . ." It is a well-known legend in Kent County that the ghost of Mary Stuart walks each year on the anniversary of her death. Some locals still visit the gravesite on that evening, run their fingers across the top of the curved stone marker, and make a wish, while others offer a toast in Mary's honor.

Reflecting on White House Farm and the longevity of its legends, one gets a feeling that Mary Perkins Stuart, George Washington, the unknown young girl on horseback, and the blue-nightgowned phantom might still be there, somewhere in that state between where they ought to be and where they want to stay.

J. J. of the Old Snow Hill Inn

The old building known as the Snow Hill Inn still stands on East Market Street in the quaint Eastern Shore town of Snow Hill, Maryland. The original section of the building had been a home built in the 1790s, and it was enlarged to its present size by 1850. One portion in the rear had served as the Snow Hill Post Office, and for a time during the recent past, the building was a Mexican restaurant. Over the coming years the place will probably change hands several more times. Up until a few years ago, some visitors staying overnight at the historic inn reported unusual sightings, and eventually they learned the story of its resident ghost.

The legend, which remains a favorite of long-time residents, was easy to discover: The former owners had mounted a framed article on the wall inside the entrance area of the building. The piece, entitled "The Ghost WithInn" by staff writer Jean Marbella with photos by Mike Lutzky, appeared in the *Baltimore Sun* on August 14, 1993, and spotlighted the exploits of a ghost affectionately referred to as "J. J."

During a visit in 1995, the innkeeper seemed not the least bit surprised when I approached with the often-asked question: "Do you really have a ghost?"

"Oh, you mean J. J.," she replied, as if talking about a relative or close friend. As she continued setting tables and cleaning the bar glasses, she casually recited a litany of events that have been attributed to the inn's ghost. These include turning lights on and off, locking doors, disturbing table settings, and knocking on the walls of her bedroom. She also indicated that the spirit "very definitely is a male presence."

When the building was first being transformed into an inn, there was extensive remodeling. One story is told of two men who were working in the building, and they could not get the window open. They had tried everything possible to pry it loose, but absolutely nothing worked, and it was becoming an issue of both personal challenge and public humiliation. Eventually, they gave up and were doing other chores in the room when the window flew up on its own and the wind started blowing in. The men, who had been given free lodging in the building as part of the work arrangement, immediately demanded to be put up someplace else. They would not stay overnight in the Snow Hill Inn.

A Towson, Maryland, attorney and her twelve-year-old son had an experience while staying in the Wicker Room in June 1993. According to the *Baltimore Sun* newspaper article, the boy was in the bathroom. When he turned around, he saw a young man, who appeared to be in his early twenties, standing across the room. And when he looked again, there was no one there. The boy knew nothing about any other unusual ghostly experiences in the inn. The woman contacted the *Baltimore Sun,* and the newspaper published the article that the owners displayed on the wall.

Perhaps the oddest and funniest incident associated with the ghost was the locked restroom door in the Victorian Lounge, when for a time it served as the inn's bar. One evening the small room was filled with regulars. Eventually, one of the customers went to the restroom door, turned and pulled on the doorknob, but it would not open. He apparently assumed that it was occupied. Time went by and others who tried were unable to gain access to the facilities, yet no one had exited from the restroom.

After more than an hour's wait and no response to several knocks on the door, the regulars got out their tools and took the locked door off its hinges. When they peered into the small room, which had no other exit door or window, it was empty. Also, the simple lock on the doorknob had not secured the door. The door had been locked by the sliding deadbolt; however, to make the deadbolt operate, one had to apply significant effort to forcefully lift the door so the bolt could be slid across to secure it properly. And someone, or something that was nowhere to be found, had secured the door.

Some suggested that the phantom that prowls the restaurant and guest rooms is William J. Aydelotte. His father was the building's primary owner, Dr. John S. Aydelotte, a prominent member of the town. According to Baltimore newspaper reports printed in December 1904, the twenty-two-year-old student at the Maryland School of Pharmacy in Baltimore was depressed over fear that he would fail an examination. In a note that was found in his rooming house, he wrote to his father stating that it is "useless to keep me at school. . . ." The young man was discovered the next day, groaning and bleeding profusely from several self-inflicted gashes across his throat. He died in the hospital, and his body was brought back to Snow Hill for burial.

No one knows for what specific reasons the son might have returned. Some believe that certain spirits will make their presence known only when they feel most comfortable with their surroundings—in this case, in his family's home. Perhaps he intends to remain with the new occupants for a very long time, staying on with each of the building's new owners indefinitely.

The Hebron Light

Sightings of a glowing and floating sphere, named the Hebron Light (but also referred to as a ghost light or spook light), have been reported for generations by Wicomico County residents in and around the small Maryland town of Hebron, located not too far from Salisbury.

But the eerie glow made major news in July 1952, when an official Maryland State Police report stated that two officers in their vehicle chased after a ten-inch glowing ball of light along a dark country road. This, however, was nothing unusual to locals, who had discussed their glowing spheres long before that incident. Theories by Wicomico residents about the mystery had included UFOs and aliens, the ghost of a slave who was hanged nearby, the phantom of a murder victim, an old railroad worker waving his lantern, the spirit of a roadside accident victim, and (of course) the skeptics' answer to nearly every unusual glow: marsh gas.

However, a look at reports in the *Salisbury Daily Times* newspaper in the summer of 1952 shows a high level of local interest in the topic. Headlines include: "Police Chase Mysterious Glow, Spooky Light Haunts Shore Road" (July 10); "Crowds Try To See

Mysterious Light" (July 11); "Curious Miss Mystery Light. It Fails To Dance Second Night in a Row" (July 12); and "Life Photographer Seeks 'Ghost Light'" (July 14). On July 16, the Associated Press ran a story with the headline "Professor Believes Ghost Light Is Gas," and the events also received space in the *Baltimore Sun.* In one local newspaper story, the light was described as "being about the size of a washbasin, about the height of an automobile light, and about the same color as a headlight. The phantom light dances around the wooded road, bounces into the woods on one side, and crosses into the nearby field."

After word spread, crowds of up to three hundred persons gathered, some with sandwiches and beer, all hoping to get a glimpse of the light. But one trooper wasn't surprised when the light didn't show, attributing the nonappearance to the size of the mob clogging the narrow back road.

A half century has passed, and progress and development have consumed a fair portion of the woods and wetlands. Subsequently, reports began to taper off toward the end of the last century. But proving the Hebron Light can still spark some interest, *Baltimore Sun* reporter Fredrick N. Rasmussen featured the mystery in his 2005 Halloween column under the headline "The Ghostly Light that Spooked Hebron." In his article, he reviewed the events of the 1952 sightings, offering details that probably have rekindled interest in the mysterious glow, and I would expect that additional reports of "spook light" sightings are bound to occur again.

The Heavy Bible

A well-known tale in Worcester County is the legend of the Heavy Bible. Apparently, it is impossible to remove the holy book from an old historic church, where the ancient text remains opened and rests on a stand in the front of the church building, near the center altar.

Anyone who tries to take the Good Book from its proper place and move it out of its house of worship will find that they've set upon an impossible task. The tale is that the holy book gets heavier and heavier as it is moved father away from its proper site. One tale tells of two young boys who broke into the church and could not move the book, even though they both tried to lift it off its stand.

On another occasion, a group of men placed the book in a wheelbarrow. As they got father from the front of the church, the contents of the wheelbarrow became so heavy that the wheeled cart broke. The perpetrators, with some initial difficulty, picked up the Bible and carried it back to its original position. As they did so, the book got lighter as it neared the altar.

Identifying which old church is the site of this spell remains a bit of a mystery, depending on whom you ask and where they reside. Some swear the Bible is in the old brick church at Showell, near the town of Bishopville. Others say the church in question used to stand in a village that is now a ghost town, and that the abandoned church building was moved and is now part of the showcase village in historic Furnace Town, located near Snow Hill. Still others say that when the old church was moved, the spell was broken so there is no longer any truth to the tale.

Another twist on this story places the Heavy Bible in a church somewhere near Cambridge in Wicomico County. However, this version is a bit more sinister, stating that the holy building was taken over by a secretive cult that conducted improper rituals. As a result, the one *being* that can remove the satanic Bible from this building is the coven's leader—the Devil.

Soldiers Sighted in the Sky

"Visions in the Air" is the front-page headline of an article that appeared on October 6, 1881, in Wilmington, Delaware's *The Morning News*. Just below, in smaller size letters, is the statement: "Soldiers and Angels Seen in the Sky." The last section of the headline reads: "The Strange Appearances as Described by Eye Witnesses in Various Parts of the Peninsula."

The article announced:

> Peninsula People have been seeing ghosts and supernatural objects with alarming frequency during the last three weeks. . . . As usual, it is not the rich man, but the poor man and his children, who have seen these supernatural images and ghost-like goblins in the air.
>
> The first instance of things heavenly having been seen, comes from Royal Oak, Maryland, a small village. . . . A little girl, some

three weeks ago, saw after nightfall, before the moon was fairly up over the horizon, whole platoons of angels slowly marching and counter-marching to and fro in the clouds, their white robes and helmets glistening with a weird light. At intervals the heavenly visitors would dance mournfully, as if to the sound of unseen music, and certainly unheard music. She rushed in to her parents and declared that the heavens had been spread. . . .

Her father, to satisfy his doubting mind, went out and was rewarded with a sight of the unearthly spectacle. The news of the mystery quickly spread from mouth to mouth, house to house, and in an incredibly short space of time the inhabitants were out en masse gazing in open-mouthed astonishment, while the white robed hosts, seemingly offended at the immense amount of genuine astonishment and wonder they were unearthing, slowly faded from sight, leaving Royal Oak a firm believer, from the little girl who was first on the spot, to the squire in his little office behind the church, in ghosts and winged goblins. But the phenomena seems to have been especially manifest in Sussex County, Delaware.

The article goes on to report that a farmer in a county southeast of Royal Oak "saw at a time almost identical with the appearance of the vision at Royal Oak, bands of soldiers of great size, equipped with dazzling uniforms, their musket steels quivering and shimmering in the pale weird light that seemed to be everywhere, marching with military precision. . . .

"In Talbot County the illusion was seen by numbers. A farmer living near Clara's Point, on going out into his yard after dark saw, as he related it afterwards to his neighbors, angels and soldiers marching side by side in the clouds, wheeling, and going through every evolution with military precision and absolutely life-like and natural." Several other comments from other observers are included in the article. The newspaper was surprised to receive numerous reports from across the Delmarva Peninsula, and it described the situation as "very singular," apparently its terminology for unusual or eerie.

It verified that there were no organized military exercises within one hundred miles of the sightings. However, two possible solutions to the visual dilemma were suggested. The first was that the events were connected to the recent death during the previous month (September 19, 1881) of the martyred President Garfield. The other was that the sighting was a reflection of the reenactment of the Revolutionary War march toward Yorktown (originally one hundred years earlier, October 6–19, 1781) being conducted in connection with the event's centennial celebration. However, the paper noted, "It [the reenactor unit] recently marched through lower Pennsylvania, and is now too far away to cast such a long shadow." Despite these and other less noteworthy attempts at explanations, the paper concluded, "There has thus far, however, been no satisfactory solution given to the series of mysterious specters in the sky."

Serial Killer and Ghost

When famous or *infamous* personalities reside along state borders, it's quite common for both jurisdictions to claim the person as its own. Such is the case of the Delmarva Peninsula's most notorious serial killer—an evil woman who lived along the Maryland-Delaware border of the Mason-Dixon Line in the early 1800s and who is said to have buried several dozen bodies in her basement and on her property. Patty Cannon was her name, and murder was her game.

From her home headquarters at the three-way crossroads called Reliance, Maryland—still located where Delaware Route 20 meets the Maryland state line, west of Seaford—Patty ran an inn that took in travelers. Since there were no Holiday Inns, Days Inns, or Marriott Suites in those days, travelers were directed to whichever area home was willing to host strangers for the night. And Patty was more than willing. In fact, "eager" would be a better word to describe her inclination to host those passing through the region.

It was well known that the Reliance hostess was generous with referral fees, so local ferrymen and merchants directed folks to Patty's overnight lodging, and some knew the travelers would vanish after their hostess served them their last meal. Patty murdered her visitors and disposed of their bodies. Then after dividing up the victims' belongings, horses, and money, she waited for the arrival of her next guests.

Of course, people noticed that more people were going into Patty's house than coming out. But they couldn't do anything about it because of the Mason-Dixon Line. Patty's home was in Maryland, but her barn (a very short walk across the dirt road) was located in

Delaware. When the local Maryland county sheriff was heading toward Reliance to investigate a reported murder, Patty would walk across the road, lean against her barn in Delaware, and wave to the lawman. Likewise, when a deputy came down the road from Sussex County, Delaware, Patty would move over to her porch in Maryland and shout obscenities across the border road. Another version of the legend reports that Patty had a line of brass nails running along her living room floor that designated the state line division. She could sit in her Maryland or Delaware chair by strolling across the room, but most believe that to be a bit of an exaggeration. Patty benefited from the reluctance of lawmen to cross state lines to chase down a criminal, and there was no communication via radio or walkie-talkie. Also, with one or two constables to work crimes in an entire county on horseback, the respective state's peace officers had plenty of work concentrating on other lawbreakers who couldn't hopscotch state boundaries.

Today the media frequently report serial killers, but in the early 1800s, reports like Patty's crimes were rather uncommon. Being a woman, she was considered a "monster" and the "personification of evil." Those descriptions were the result of documented reports that she also murdered children. In one instance it is said she cooked a live baby in her fireplace. (Patty found the infant's constant crying annoying.)

Eventually, Maryland and Delaware coordinated Patty's capture, and she was held in the basement of the Georgetown, Delaware, Courthouse for trial. In 1829, one can imagine the excitement and festivities associated with Patty's capture and expected hanging. Vendors, selling food and Patty Cannon hanging dolls, set out their wares in the center of Georgetown. Hundreds of citizens lined up to get a seat in the courtroom, and many hundreds more prepared to travel from surrounding counties of nearby states to witness the public execution. But Patty ruined the party.

On the night before her trial was to begin, Patty swallowed arsenic that she kept in the hem of her dress (having already used the fine powder as a method to dispose of two husbands) and committed suicide. No trial, no hanging, no fair, and no buyers for the food and crafts. The disappointed crowd left cursing the serial killer, and no one claimed the body. Patty was placed in the town's paupers' field behind the Sussex County Courthouse, and immediately

locals began spreading tales that her ghost roamed Reliance and Federalsburg in Maryland or, at times, along the Nanticoke River and in the cells of the Georgetown jail. Most thought that was the end of the Patty Cannon story.

Not quite.

In the early 1900s, town officials decided to enlarge the courthouse. They hired locals to unearth the decomposed bodies from behind the building and move the paupers' field and its weathered coffins and remains to another site. A boy, who had been hired to work the excavation, pulled up Patty's remains, reached inside her coffin, and stole the murderess's skull. At the end of the workday, he took the noggin home and handed it to his father. The enterprising youngster's proud parent promptly placed the peculiar prize on a nail in his barn, and he showed it off for all to see—charging visitors two bits (25 cents) to rub it for good luck and make a wish. Over subsequent generations, Patty Cannon's eerie skull was handed down through the family as a treasured heirloom, for a time resting on the mantel of a lawyer's office. But in the 1960s, the skull's owner, who was leaving the area and heading out west, donated this particular prized piece of Patty to the care of the Dover, Delaware, library. And there it remains to this day.

In a red vinyl hatbox, Patty's skull is tucked safely away, but available for anyone to see. I have held what's left of Patty in my hands, and during two Halloween storytelling programs I had the honor to share the stage with the infamous murderess, who remained silent while resting on a black-velvet-covered table surrounded by flickering candles.

There is much more to Patty's tale of murder and hidden treasure, of nightriders and kidnappings. In the years before Harriet Tubman was guiding escaped slaves north through Delmarva's marshes, forests, and rivers toward the Mason-Dixon Line and freedom, Patty Cannon and her nightriders were conducting a reverse Underground Railroad that headed south, instead of north. Since the slave trade was legally abolished in 1808, Patty and her gang were making big money by kidnapping freedmen—former slaves who had legally purchased their freedom—or escaped slaves and reselling them to slave traders from the Deep South when they visited Patty's compound near the banks of the Nanticoke River. Essentially, the murderess was getting rich by sending these poor souls back into slavery and making thousands of dollars—in the 1820s—on each transaction.

Depending on one's point of view at the time, Patty was feared, hated, glorified, useful, or despised. But her story is true; she did exist, and a Maryland state historical marker stands in the front yard of what is believed to be the site of her old home at the Reliance crossroads.

And while Patty has been the subject of documentaries, books, and countless tales, perhaps a Sussex County builder has provided the most unusual anecdote related to the centuries-old Patty Cannon legend. For along River Road south of Reliance, near the Delaware-Maryland border and Woodland Ferry, stands a development with a green and white sign proclaiming: "Patty Cannon Estates." As one local remarked, "It's like living in Charles Manson Manor. I wonder how many of the current residents realize their neighborhood is named after a serial killer?"

Haunted Horses

Even though Kentucky seems to get all the publicity, Maryland is considered one of the best thoroughbred-breeding regions in the world, being the home of a such legends as Kentucky Derby winners War Admiral (1937) and Northern Dancer (1964).

A large number of horse-breeding and training farms are located in Cecil County, and most are clustered on rolling, scenic acreage just south of the Chesapeake & Delaware Canal.

To maintain operations, there is a small army of trainers, grooms, horse movers, veterinarians, jockeys, and landowners. The horse handlers get to work very early, while it's still dark, and they are well into their work routine at sunrise, when the layer of morning mist is still hanging low against the ground.

Horse workers tend to be superstitious, and some admit that the morning darkness can play tricks on their senses. Some even believe that ghost horses have appeared in the fog, sometimes accompanied by the spirits of workers who had spent considerable time many years ago in the old barns and stables.

In a few cases, the apparitions appear to be very real, and some have even waved a "hello" to present-day staff—before the ghost visitors suddenly disappear after passing by. Another farm legend is associated with the Ghost Mare drinking all the water from the troughs, but others suggest the more practical explanation involving low water pressure or someone forgetting to do his job. But those who discount the ghostly horse stories admit even they don't have an explanation for the consistency in the descriptions of the sightings, particularly by new workers who have no knowledge of previous eerie incidents.

A long-time worker suggested that it might be the roving spirit of an employee of the estate, maybe someone who was so comfortable with his surroundings that he doesn't want to move on. "The wealthy people who own the farm had lifetime employees, who were there forever," the worker said. "Maybe when this old worker died, he just stuck around 'cause that's all he knew. He was dedicated to the end, and when the end came, he just stuck around to make sure the horses were cared for properly. That's my opinion."

That might account for the handler, but what about the Ghost Mare and other restless, spirited horses? According to several sources, horse graveyards are common on the training facilities and horse farms on the Eastern Shore and elsewhere. Carved gravestones and metal plaques bear the names of million-dollar money winners. On some farms, tall trees and landscaped shrubbery are used to mark the final resting places of famous racehorses and other less well-known, but equally loved, animals. Burial ceremonies at horse cemeteries can cause the owners and workers to break down in tearful good-byes.

"I've been there when they bury horses," one worker said. "I've assisted in putting them in the grave, and I've cried and shed some tears myself. You look around and even the roughest, toughest barn crew are brushing away tears from their eyes. To me, and others, it's hard when some of them have to be put down because of age or arthritis problems. Usually, the end is made as easy as possible. A lot of the horses are really loved. It's like putting down a dog or a cat; it's just bigger.

"The spot is selected; gravestones are put down after the ground settles. It all depends on what the owners want to do. On most of the farms, there's an area marked off as a special place for the animals they loved . . . a pet cemetery or horse graveyard. They call it by different names.

"But I love this job. The smell is terrible, the weather is harsh, but the horses. . . . Wow. When they look at you and they say thanks, you know it's all worth it. You see it in their eyes, or they'll put a head on your shoulder and give you a hug when they know you've helped them out. The horses talk to you in their own way. You look at a horse's eyes, and you know what they're saying. But, I heard this saying once, and it's very true. 'If you work with livestock, you're going to work with dead stock.' It's just a fact of life."

OUTstanding Halloween Custom

Fifty-one weeks a year, Rising Sun is a quiet community resting amidst scenic farmland on the northern edge of the Delmarva Peninsula. But during Halloween week, as one long-time resident put it, "All hell used to break out."

To hear the old-timers tell it, the annual shenanigans started around 1900. Townsfolk used to head out into the countryside and pick up farm machinery, porch furniture, rocking chairs, cornhusks, and loads of manure. Then they'd dump it all, right smack dab beneath the town's circle and lone traffic light, in front of the old National Bank of Rising Sun. Talk to locals in the heart of town, and they will share some tales of antics and items they have witnessed passing by their front porches during Mischief Night and Halloween evening, particularly a fair number of outhouses.

That's right, since the 1920s, privies—outdoor toilets, of the old-fashioned, wooden Johnny-on-the-spot variety—have become the unknown haulers' object of choice. Most years in the last two decades, sometime after dark the "borrowed" goods would appear in the town's major crossroads with a dependability that would put many Federal Express couriers to shame. Town officials have acknowledged the practice and one added, "It depends on the availability of outhouses. Today, they are getting to be few and far between."

Years ago the anonymous donors would drop off the outhouse directly under the town's lone red light and take off. Occasionally, they would set it on fire. But today they tend to be more considerate and place the wooden privy on the edge of the street on the sidewalk, and they don't usually try to set it aflame. Of course, as with all folk traditions, no one can pinpoint who started the annual outhouse delivery.

Part of the event's mystery is that no one knows who drops off the wooden outhouse, but it is assumed that for many years local teenagers were, and still are, responsible. But even the older folks seem to get into the game—sort of like a family tradition that's been rolling along through several generations. What's particularly amazing is that such an unusual custom continues into the twenty-first century, and in some cases it has expanded into a two-evening event. During a few years, outhouses were deposited on both Mischief Night and Halloween evening.

While the exact time of the delivery is a guarded secret, police and townsfolk keep an eye out beginning anytime after dark. And on rare occasions, local law enforcement officials have been tipped off and were waiting at the edge of town. But in recent times, instead of apprehending these phantom privy perpetrators, the officials have provided the roving outhouse dumpers with a "police escort."

Of course, such a bizarre custom has tons of local legends and tall tales that get longer and taller as the years go by. One is about the town drunk who used the outhouse as a bathroom while it was sitting under the red light; then there was an unfortunate fellow who had an outhouse fall on him as he was trying to remove it from a farm and then fell headfirst into the sewage pit; and there was the year a farmer locked himself inside his outhouse and allowed the boys to carry it all the way into town, but then he stepped out with his gun and said, "All right, boys, let's take it back."

One autumn many years ago, the mayor vowed to "stop the annual mischief" and hired off-duty detectives from Wilmington or Baltimore (depending upon who you talk to) to end the deplorable actions. The locals told the hired-gun carpetbaggers to get out of town, but when the big-city cops tried to leave Rising Sun, they found all their tires were flat. The detectives were quoted as saying, "Them people up there's crazy!"

Crazy or not, and ready or not, each Halloween there's a good chance the outhouse will arrive in the center of Rising Sun. And on the edge of the action, locals and visitors, with digital cameras and camcorders in hand, will be waiting to capture this unusual, silly, and uniquely Delmarva custom.

Bigg Lizz

Her name is Bigg Lizz. She's so big that we spell it with two "g's" and two "z's," out of respect for and recognition of her extraordinary life, untimely death, and apparent immortality. For some believe that Bigg Lizz still roams the swamps and forests of Dorchester County even though she died more than 150 years ago.

The legend of Bigg Lizz has been told in country stores, repeated in barbershops, written up for school papers, and documented in newspapers and books about regional folklore. One of the most well-known versions of the tale can be found in *Shore Folklore, Growing Up With Ghosts, 'N Legends, 'N Tales, 'N Home Remedies* by The Old Honker Thomas A. Flowers. But this account of the Bigg Lizz tale has been assembled from various stories in books and magazines, plus verbal versions of the famous Delmarva folktale.

During the Civil War, citizens throughout the Delmarva Peninsula were divided. Some were loyal to the North, while others had equally strong sentiments for the Southern cause. Neighbors were at odds over the issues of slavery and states' rights, and members of the same family with opposite views found some sons wearing blue uniforms and others fighting in gray. While Maryland remained in the Union, many of her citizens on both sides of the Chesapeake Bay fought for and supported the Confederacy. In Dorchester County, a wealthy plantation owner worked secretly as a Rebel agent.

Sacks of gold and silver coin were delivered to his plantation, where Bigg Lizz worked. "The Master" considered her one of his most dependable and hardworking slaves, but he eventually learned Bigg Lizz was a Union spy. Since he had treated her quite well, the Master was very disappointed that she had been reporting his clandestine activities to Federal troops on a regular basis.

One night, when his chest was filled and could not contain any more gold coin, the Master called for Bigg Lizz—a very large black woman with powerful muscles—and he directed her to place the wooden trunk in the back of his wagon. Together they rode in darkness on a moonless summer night into the depths of Green Briar Swamp. Once there, the Master tossed Bigg Lizz a shovel and ordered her to dig a hole deep enough to hide the large fortune-filled chest. As Bigg Lizz burrowed deeper, less and less of her body emerged from the growing hole. Up and down she went, over and over. The rhythm of her powerful body took on a steady beat. When the hole was dug to the Master's satisfaction, he ordered Lizz to place the massive box in the bottom of the pit. That done, Lizz resumed her shovel work, returning the fresh pile of damp earth into the deep hole.

Busy with her task, Bigg Lizz didn't notice the Master, standing above on the wagon deck, directly behind her body. He clutched a large tobacco knife, razor sharp and about three feet long, with both hands. As her body bent forward, then raised itself into an upright position, Bigg Lizz's massive sweating head was only a few feet from the Master's waist. He tapped his toe, getting into the rhythm of the moment, her rhythm, her steady pace. Then, when her head was highest and closest to the level of his belt line, he pulled back both arms and directed the silver blade forward, connecting with Bigg Lizz's neck. A strange look of surprise was frozen on her face as the round, full head flew into the air and landed with a "thunk" against a nearby tree. Within seconds, Bigg Lizz ceased to function, and her lifeless mass landed atop the chest of Confederate gold.

With the crypt conveniently prepared and the gold safely hidden, the Master adjusted his riding gloves and began to fill in the hole. This was one physical task he could trust no one else to do. Slowly, Bigg Lizz was covered with swamp dirt. Laughing aloud, the Master thought how clever it was for him to leave the slave's body sprawled atop the treasure. With satisfaction, he compared her eternal role to the ancient pirate practice where a murdered crewmember was tossed atop a hidden treasure to safeguard its precious contents for eternity.

Then he remembered the woman's head—the surprised face that had rolled off and hit the moss-covered tree. Stopping his horses, he turned in his seat and thought for a moment about going back and retrieving the noggin. But in the dark it would be impossible to locate. Besides, a wild boar or fox would cart off the tasty face, and all evidence of his treasure and the murder would vanish before daylight.

It was nearly three o'clock in the morning when he arrived at the front of his mansion. Quite tired from a full evening of stressful activity, the Master was in bed by 3:15 A.M. and fast asleep moments later. After what seemed to be only a few seconds, he was awakened by a scratching sound that seemed to be coming from a corner of the room. He turned in his bed, pulled the pillow close around his head and ears to block out the sound, and tried to return to his much needed sleep. But rest would not be his that night. The annoyance was louder this time and sounded closer, much closer. It was as if the scratching was coming from above his mattress.

Sitting up in his bed, the Master shouted, "What is making such a noise?"

No one answered, but he noticed that the temperature in his room had dropped dramatically. It had been a humid summer night, but in his room it felt like the winter winds had entered through the open third-floor window. Jumping from his bed to shut the shutters, his bare feet reacted to the bitter cold of the floor, but he never reached the window. From the corner of his eye, he noticed two small yellow dots of light. They were about four feet off the floor and moving toward him. As they came closer, a huge figure of a woman in familiar clothing—worker's clothing, slave clothing—came into view.

Bigg Lizz emerged from the shadows. Her headless body glided across the room toward the Master, who was moving backwards at a very rapid pace. In the dead woman's left hand was her head, which she held by her hair. The yellow glowing eyes seemed to direct the rest of Bigg Lizz's immense dead body in the direction it should go. She had no trouble following her prey around the mansion's large master bedroom. In the ghost's right hand was a rather impressive tobacco knife. The Master knew that its blade was sharp, for he had used it recently with good results. However, now the bright metal was coated with dried, black-red stains—the blood of Bigg Lizz, who had returned from the swamp to take her revenge.

The Master was a smart man, knew more than most. After all, he owned and operated a successful plantation, and he had convinced his Rebel associates to trust him with much of their personal wealth. So he must have known that his death would occur in a matter of moments and that there would be no reasoning with or mercy coming from the angry ghoul. But logic does not always prevail in times of strife and danger. The Master pleaded and cried, shouted and cursed, but nothing swayed the vengeful ghost. Terrified at the thought of spending eternity without his head, the Master leaped out the window, crashing to his death on the ground

three stories below. His body was found the following morning, and he was buried on the grounds of his plantation.

The chest of gold and Bigg Lizz's head and body were never located. According to legend, her banshee remains in the swamp, somewhere in the area of Bucktown, south of Cambridge near DeCoursey's Bridge. She's there to protect the gold, a solitary sentinel standing watch forever. Treasure hunters with sophisticated metal detectors have visited the area searching for the lost fortune. They say they're not interested in or afraid of Bigg Lizz. Some even laugh when they hear stories about her role as the "guardian of the gold." But they're careful to work only during daylight.

Area high school students, who say she's the product of an active imagination, have organized outings to locate the swamp monster. But they make only one excursion into the forests. When they speak about the experience, they admit the marshes are eerie, very troubling, and not a nice place to play or explore. But each year newcomers arrive to search and to see for themselves. Some call them "legend trippers," hoping to get a glimpse of the monster. Others just refer to them as "crazy teenagers out for a night of fun."

There are even reports that Bigg Lizz has moved. One story tells of her head appearing in the Chesapeake Bay, circling small pleasure boats at night and calling out for help, asking to be pulled from the water. Another version says that the old girl has taken the treasure with her and that she now sits on the chest in the middle of the Pocomoke Forest. But that story seems a bit far-fetched, not as believable as the original tale.

But who's to say what's true and what's not, what's real and what's imagined, what's the way it is and what's the way you want it to be? The facts are these: Bigg Lizz was real. She was murdered. The Master is dead. The gold remains to be found. And even in the twenty-first century, strange and terrifying things still happen deep in the swamps and forests on the Eastern Shore of Maryland.

Indian Ghosts Under the Jail

The tiny peninsula that formed where the Little Elk Creek and the Big Elk Creek meet southwest of Elkton is an interesting geographical and historical site. The land near the convergence of the two streams attracted the attention of the Cecil County government when it decided to build a new detention center on the marshy wet-lands in the early 1980s.

Some folks, however, believed the location had been a popular site for centuries. A group of area archaeologists arranged to make exploratory digs before construction began to determine if the long-held belief that an Indian village had been located there was cor-rect. When members of the Northeast Chapter of the Archaeological Society of Maryland and the staff of Mid-Atlantic Archaeological Research did excavations on the thirteen-acre site, what they found was interesting. Their efforts uncovered hundreds of pieces of American Indian pottery, more than one hundred arrowheads, and, about four feet below the surface, a skeleton in a grave. The human bones were sent to the Smithsonian Institution, which returned a report dating the remains to be from about AD 1400. Encouraged by their success, the archaeological team continued its efforts and found more gravesites. Their locations were logged in, noted, and left undisturbed.

Their exploration verified that the small peninsula had been the site of a large Indian village and burial ground. Even hundreds of years ago the convergence of the two creeks was recognized as being a good location to establish a settlement, for it was easier than other open spaces to defend, and the water routes encouraged accessibility and trade. Also, years later in the early 1800s, the area was the site of Fort Hollingsworth, which served as both a trading post for settlers and a military outpost for the Maryland militia.

After the archaeological procedures were completed and docu-mentation recorded, construction on the new jail began. In the sum-mer of 1984, the Cecil County Detention Center, operated by the Cecil County Sheriff's Office, was officially opened. It was common knowledge that the prison was built in the vicinity of an Indian burial ground. In fact, for some time the main wing of the new building had a display of arrowheads and Indian tools and pottery found in the area.

In the last few months before the prison was ready to accept its first occupants, correctional staff were assigned to stay overnight to maintain security and keep the curious away. Jane, who has worked for the sheriff's office, heard stories from night shift workers who said they were bothered by unexplained footsteps, saw lights go on and off, and heard howling sounds that seemed to be rushing through the halls of the empty center. It was during the early days at the new facility, when the prison population was well below its 128-person capacity, that Jane learned of a very unusual experience.

With only about eighty-five prisoners, each inmate was able to have his own four- by eight-foot cell. Mike, a small-time criminal serving time for a light offense, was assigned during the day to out-of-cell duty cleaning offices. "This guy was no wimp," Jane said, thinking back on the incident. "He was in his mid-twenties, used to associate with bikers, and he was a big guy, six foot and two hundred pounds. He came into the office and looked scared. I said, 'What's wrong, Mike?'"

She said that he looked around, as if he wanted to make sure no one could hear him. "You're not going to believe this," he told Jane, and then went on to explain.

After the usual 11 P.M. lockdown the night before, Mike said he fell asleep and was awakened in the wee hours of the morning. While his eyes adjusted to the dark, he noticed that he couldn't move his arms. They were pinned down, tight against his body, by the hands of an Indian chief who was straddling the prisoner's body and pressing down hard against him.

"Mike said the Indian was wearing a bonnet full of feathers and war paint," Jane said. "He tried to move and wrestled with the spirit, and said he ended up struggling with the ghost for most of the night, until daylight. He said there never was any talk between them. But he was really afraid, to the point that he asked to be moved into a different cell with another guy. He said he felt better at night with someone else around."

Jane said Mike never saw the Indian again, and no one else admitted to seeing the warrior either. "It was so real to him," she said. "When people say, 'He looks like he's seen a ghost!' that was the case, here. He was so pale, and it was obvious that he had a rough night. It was hard, really something, for him to admit what happened. He wasn't the kind that wanted anybody to think he was afraid. I don't think he ever went into that cell again. It didn't bother him to walk by it during the day, but at night, he wouldn't go near it."

Not far from the prison, Oldfield Point Road runs along the Elk River. Until recently, it was a quiet, unnoticed area of the county, a bit off the beaten path—visited by boat people in the summer and home to only a few year-round residents who lived in small cottages by the water's edge. Now, passersby can see growing areas of residential development as more commuters discover the scenic setting and the calming, picturesque views of the nearby Elk River. What rests nearby or even beneath some of the newer properties is questionable. Residents of certain homes in the area have reported seeing circles of fire and hearing chanting in the late evenings. No logical explanation has been found. Rumors and hearsay, however, suggest that the answer may be that some home sites are located uncomfortably close to more undiscovered Indian burial grounds. It's not an impossibility.

Hand Nailed to a Tree

Until a few generations ago, reports of lynchings were not uncommon across the Delmarva Peninsula. In the early 1900s outside Wilmington, Delaware, at the northern border of the region, a mob broke into a prison, pulled the accused from captivity, burned him at a stake, and then distributed his bones among the crowd.

In 1863, in Caroline County, a similar event occurred. In the midst of the days of the Civil War, a Denton area man was accused of the murder of a young girl, but the suspect never received a fair trial. Instead, he was strung up and lynched by a local mob and then his hand was chopped off and nailed to a tree.

In his book *Now This Is the Truth . . . and Other Lies,* well-known Delmarva author and folklorist Hal Roth tells the thoroughly researched tale in his chapter entitled "A Lynched Man's Hand."

One fall evening, twelve-year-old Ellen Plummer didn't return home to her farm near Greensborough. The next morning, her body was found in a wooded area. She had been sexually assaulted and murdered.

Jim Wilson, a twenty-three-year-old mulatto who worked at a nearby farm, was arrested. As he was being taken to the Denton jail, eight miles away, area farmers grabbed the prisoner and hanged him from a tree by his thumbs until he "confessed" to the murder. Somewhat satisfied, the crowd allowed the sheriff to lock the prisoner in the town jail, but after three days a restless mob stormed the building, broke down the door, threw a rope about Wilson's neck, and dragged him outside of town.

Stopping at a tree near the courthouse, the mob hoisted the lifeless body into the air and then proceeded to shoot it until it fell to the ground. The second stop for Wilson's corpse was near an African-American church, but a local saloon keeper convinced the gang to take the body further down the road, as a swinging corpse too close to his establishment would be bad for the inn's business.

The mob agreed and headed into a nearby valley, where the rowdy bunch started a fire. Meanwhile, a Delaware butcher—who had brought along the tools of his trade—began chopping off Wilson's limbs to the delight of the crowd that was singing, dancing, and out of control.

As Roth notes in his book, a reporter on the scene wrote: "The orgies enacted around the blazing faggots would have been deemed disgraceful by savages."

One of the participants pulled Wilson's burning hands from the fire and nailed one to a nearby tree. When his wife made a humorous remark, he threw the other hand in her lap, and she immediately tossed it back into the fire.

When summarizing the aftermath of the melee, Roth observed: "Although many good citizens of Delmarva denounced the atrocity, no witness was willing to step forward and testify before a grand jury, and not a single perpetrator ever felt the hand of human justice. But . . . a vengeful, higher fist served fearsome retribution."

Within twenty-four hours of the gruesome and murderous festival, the woman who had joked and tossed Wilson's hand into the fire suffered paralysis of the arm she had used. Shortly afterwards, her husband was shot in the lungs while trying to rob a black man and died of pneumonia.

The Delaware butcher lost his customers, who were concerned that he used the same knives to cut his meat as he did to carve up Jim Wilson. To add to his injuries, while at a railroad station in nearby Seaford, the butcher fell under a train and had his right arm severed; and later, in a drunken state, he fell into the Nanticoke River and drowned—despite the fact that several people were standing nearby who witnessed his plight and could have saved him.

According to reports and oral history, folks near Denton commented that nearly everyone associated with the violent murder of Jim Wilson died suddenly, violently, in agony, or in poverty.

On April 30, 1883, a writer for the Denton, Maryland, *Journal* wrote:

> I drove out to a tree, four miles from the village, which still bears the imprint of the hand of a Negro, which was nailed there by one of the mob that handed, quartered, mutilated, and burned him nearly twenty years ago. This singular freak of nature, or sign manual of divine displeasure, as many residents of the county esteem it, is generally treated with such contemptuous disbelief by strangers visiting Caroline County that it is difficult to find one who has seen it willing to talk about it, but an official of the county, who did his full duty in an endeavor to stay the fury of the mob, consented to show me the remarkable tree. It is a giant swamp poplar, quite three feet in diameter, standing close by the road that opens up Tuckahoe Neck, the garden spot of the country. About twelve feet from the ground, on the road face of the tree, is a seeming scar, which might attract a casual glance on account of its marked difference in color from the other bark. Probably a stranger would not notice the singular tracing of which it is a frame, but to one looking for it, the outline of a human hand, somewhat elongated by the growth of the tree, grows as one looks until it takes almost the very similitude of the withering hand that was nailed there twenty years ago. Even the nail is still visible, although the bark has grown beyond so that it is half an inch below the surface. The tracking of the hand appears in a much smoother as well as light colored bark—the palm through which the nail was driven being clearest in shape, with the thumb and spread index and little finger scarcely less perceptible. My guide said the appearance grows more noticeable with each year, and it would be difficult to persuade him that it was not due to other than providential design. It is worthy of remark, lest the imprint in the tree be attributed to some action of the decomposing animal tissue, that lumbermen working in the vicinity made up a purse and hired a man to take the hand down within a week of the time it was placed there.

And although nearly 150 years have passed since the murder and mutilation of Jim Wilson, one wonders: What became of the tree? Does it still stand? Was the hand buried unceremoniously nearby? Or, like the other remnants of his charred body, was it scattered in the forest, which eventually gave way to more modern homes, manicured yards, or a strip mall or convenience store. There are numerous unmarked graves hidden beneath today's symbols of progress, and the sites of the events related to Jim Wilson's murder and his infamous tree are only two of them.

Inn and a Barrel of Rum

There's an interesting story associated with the Inn at Mitchell House, located near Tolchester at the northern section of the Chesapeake Bay. After all, how many historic homes are able to claim a British soldier died on its kitchen table?

The fact didn't deter Jim and Tracy Stone from taking over the eighteenth-century manor house surrounded by woods and situated on a knoll overlooking ten rolling acres. In fact, the historic connection to a nearby battle adds to the home's attraction—plus the fact it was rated in the Top Ten among ten thousand inns by America's Historic Inns, Inc.

According to documents recorded in the Maryland Registry of old home sites, during the War of 1812 troops from the British warship HMS *Menelaus*, under the command of twenty-eight-year-old Sir Peter Parker, came ashore and marched through Kent County. A slave alerted the local militia, and the Americans marched from Belle Air, now known as Fairlee, and encountered the British forces at the Battle of Caulk's Field.

On August 31, 1814, the British sustained fifteen casualties, and they were forced to retreat. Carrying their seriously wounded leader, Sir Peter Parker, they headed back to their ship, which was anchored in the upper Chesapeake Bay. En route, they stopped at the Mitchell house to give the young naval officer emergency medical attention. Unfortunately, he had lost a tremendous amount of blood and died in the Mitchell house kitchen.

Afterwards, Parker's corpse was taken back to the ship. So that the officer's body could be preserved during the return voyage to England, the recently departed was placed in a barrel of white rum. It is not known if any of the *Menelaus* sailors availed themselves of the naval officer's spirited spirits during the long sea voyage back to the British Isles. Upon its return, the body was buried in St. Margaret's, adjacent to Westminster Abbey.

After the Stones took over the inn, Tracy's father, Edward O'Donnell, figured that the British government must have a portrait of Sir

Peter Parker (1785–1814). He contacted several British museums and eventually was able to secure a copy of a painting of the naval officer whose last breath was spent in Mitchell House. Today, a framed color representation of the sailor hangs prominently in the center of the inn's Parlor Number One, off the main entrance hall.

Tracy considers the story an interesting historical anecdote and noted that Kent County youngsters are taught the area legend in elementary school. Today, the home features six guest rooms, all named after local historical persons or sites, including Sir Peter Parker Room.

"He never stayed here," said Tracy, "but he died in the kitchen which is just below his room, so it seemed fitting to name the bedroom after him."

With all this history and character, one can't help but wonder if any ghosts reside within the inn's 250-year-old walls. Tracy and Jim offer knowing smiles . . . pause . . . and then begin to share their more unusual, unexplained experiences. They stress that all, or at least most, have been of a friendly nature.

The house has been an inn only since 1982. In 1986, they purchased the property, along with many of its furnishings, from the inn's former owners. A little more than a year after they had moved in, the couple visited the inn's former owners. After dinner, the previous innkeepers shared some of the strange things that had happened when they owned the Inn at Mitchell House. They said the Colonel Philip Reed Room, also referred to as Bedroom Number 4 located in the original farmhouse section, contained a rocking chair. That rocker, they said, sometimes moved back and forth by itself, without anyone in it.

Tracy admitted that she has never seen the chair rocking, but she has removed it from the room and placed it in the basement.

Why?

"It was looking a bit ragged and beat up," she said. Then, slowly raising her eyes as if embarrassed, she added, "I guess I could have fixed it, but then. . . ."

As the evening progressed, the new owners discovered that the former owners' basset hound would enjoy spending time inside that Bedroom Number 4, and it would act as if it were playing with some unknown person or perhaps another dog. Tracy said her family's cat would not go into the room as if it was afraid of what is inside.

"There have been guests who have sat in the rocking chair," said Jim, "and they claim they felt something brush against their legs, as if it were a dog ghost passing by."

One guest, Jim recalled, came out of the room one morning and said to the innkeeper, "There's something in that room, isn't there?" But Jim added that he said it very calmly, even matter-of-factly, and not upset.

Since they have owned the property, Tracy said two female psychics have stayed at the inn, each on a different occasion. She added that one psychic said there is sometimes an area where certain things are pushed toward a corner. The other psychic told the couple "the basement held something bad."

Laughing, Tracy said, "That's where my laundry room is. So it gives me an excuse not to go down there."

Jim said that until thirty years ago there were shackles that had been used to chain slaves still hanging in the basement, but they were removed and the areas had been patched over.

Sitting in Parlor Number Two, Jim and Tracy discussed the significance of their home and its character and historical value. "If the walls could talk," she said, "imagine what secrets they could share. There have been so many deaths and births in this house. And it's amazing that it has such a light, friendly atmosphere. I absolutely enjoy it. If I was remotely uncomfortable, I would have been out of here a long time ago. I've never been scared so much that it has bothered me."

"But," Jim added, "there have been a few nights that she has hit me on the side in the middle of the night and sent me downstairs to check on noises and things."

"I find it all very interesting," said Tracy. "If there is something here, whatever it is, it is nice. And it can stay here."

'Show me the way!'

In Talbot County, there's the tale of a local country doctor. I've been told this story took place in the 1700s before the days leading up to the Revolution. Another source said the events occurred immediately after the Civil War. Yet a third taleteller swore the story happened during Victorian times. While I have no idea, with certainty, when the event happened (and apparently neither does anyone else), the essence of the tale in all three versions goes something like this.

In the countryside outside of Easton, a certain country doctor was well known for more than his medical expertise. It was well known that the gentleman tended to drink too much, and it was accepted by patients in the region that he often conducted his practice in a less than sober state. However, because he was proficient at his profession—and since there was no other doctor in the area to offer any competition—the locals were tolerant of the old physician's tendency to set a broken bone even if it was obvious that he had recently "tied one on."

Late one evening, a good friend of the doctor was seriously injured while cleaning his gun. When a nervous stranger awakened the physician at his office/home and told him of the tragic accident, the healer was in a seriously tipsy state. Knowing he must do all he could to save his friend, the old doc staggered to his barn, hitched up his faithful horse, and headed off in his buggy at top speed. However, since he was pretty well sloshed, the doctor's sense of direction was nonexistent. In the darkness and in his confused state, he became lost. By the time he arrived at his friend's home, the wounded man had died. After the demise of his friend, the doctor was never the same. To erase his sense of guilt and shame, he drank even more heavily than before the tragedy. Eventually, late one night, while riding along a narrow back road—probably feeling no pain—the old doctor's horse and carriage wandered off the road, and he was killed.

Although the doctor is believed to be buried in the Old White Marsh Episcopal Church cemetery, many believe that his guilty, intoxicated soul cannot rest. According to the most repeated version of the tale, at various times of the year, locals have reported hearing the galloping of an invisible horse. Still others have said they can hear a ghostly voice shouting, "Show me the way! I'm lost! Quickly! Show me the way!"

Screaming Polly

"She roams the banks of the Bohemia River."

"No. She floats across the river."

"I've seen her ghost in the fog, along Light Road north of Warwick."

"I think my grandmother said she froze to death out on the state land, near Fair Hill."

"She was originally from Cecilton or Hacks Point."

"Warwick was her home, before she and her baby got lost in a blizzard and froze to death in the snow. That's why she can't rest."

Seeking to solve the mystery of Screaming Polly—who she was, the circumstances of her death and/or disappearance, and where her spirit continues to roam—has proven difficult, if not impossible. Many southern Cecil countians have claimed to hear the female phantom screeching at night somewhere south of the Bohemia River and north of the village of Cecilton.

The details of her ghost story are as varied as pinpointing the location of Polly's howling and her haunting grounds, but the most popular version describes her as a young servant who became the love interest of a wealthy county landowner. However, when the aristocrat learned that Polly was "with child," he banished her from his mansion. Stories abound about the plight of the pregnant servant, who roamed back roads and villages, knocking on the doors of slaves and townsfolk alike, seeking shelter for herself and her unborn child. Since everyone was afraid of the master's anger, no one offered Polly aid. She's believed to have died in a blizzard, screaming for help, " . . . and every time there is a snowstorm, her chilling cries are heard to this very day."

Legend number two involves a romantic young couple—the son of a wealthy landowner and attractive young Polly, who worked on the plantation as an indentured servant. Knowing their marriage would never be approved, the young lovers planned to elope and seek happiness and fortune in the new lands to the west.

Unfortunately, the boy's father discovered the plot and delayed his son's appearance at the rendezvous. When the young man eventually arrived, depending on your version: He found Polly dead on the side of the road, apparently run over by a carriage; he learned that Polly had left the county to live a miserable and poor life alone (or with their child); or Polly did not appear at the meeting site because she had been kidnapped and tied to a tree in the woods where she froze to death in a snowstorm. Of course, a ghostly figure in a long white gown has been seen floating across the waters of the Bohemia River and the narrow back roads of the rural farmlands.

Another long-time local resident said Polly appears on only two nights a year—Mischief Night, October 30, and Halloween, October 31. The woman recalled celebrating her October 30 birthday many years ago by traveling with friends to "Screaming Polly Lane," located in the area of Stemmers Run Road, between Pond Neck and Grove Neck roads: On a one-lane, unpaved pathway, she and a group of friends stopped their car, shut off the lights, and performed a common ritual—flashing the headlights and sounding the horn three times. "This is when the fog came billowing in from both sides of the road, and we heard this extremely high-pitched scream," she said. "We saw a bright whitish form sort of float across the road. There was enough detail to ascertain that it was a female carrying her screaming head under her left arm." They departed the area quickly, taking only the vivid memory of a headless Screaming Polly with them. Recalling the account "still raises the hair on the back of my head," she said.

Hole in the Wall

They call it "Hole in the Wall," what's left of an abandoned church with its surrounding ancient graveyard; that's the source of many a tall tale and ghost story. Outside Easton, along Route 50, about seven miles south of its intersection with MD Route 322, the haunted place stands beside the northbound lane, at the top of a small hill. The historical marker indicates its true name: "Old White Marsh Episcopal Church." The metal plaque also offers a few other tidbits of history, but like all state makers, it shares nothing of the "good stuff." You have to search out the legends and eerie tales.

It's a small, country-type resting place, not jammed with rows and rows of markers and statues that you tend to find in today's big city and suburban cemeteries. And while its worn headstones mark the final home of some of the region's earliest settlers, the site is associated with Talbot County's most interesting haunted tale.

A woman, who died suddenly, was buried in a family plot in the graveyard beside the Old White March Episcopal Church. As the old story goes, on the evening of her burial, grave robbers opened the freshly dug grave, pried back the coffin lid, and began stealing all of the recently departed's valuables. When one robber was unable to separate an expensive ruby ring that glowed in the moonlight from the fresh corpse's finger, the robber pulled out his knife and began to cut the jewelry away. While carving off the delicate finger that was swollen under the ring, the robber moved his face close to the stubborn finger.

The sudden pain of the knife blade apparently caused the "dead" body to rise up and "come back to life." The grave robber standing above the hole was able to escape into the woods, and some say he's still running. But the thieving partner in the hole, who had been cutting on the dead woman's ring finger, wasn't as lucky. Terrified that he had awakened the dead, the grave robber stumbled back in fright. Frantic and shouting, he tried in vain to escape from the "vampire woman" and climb out of the fresh grave. In the confusion, he hit his head on the handle of the shovel while trying to escape from the awakened corpse, and the man fell into the slightly used, but still warm, coffin.

Ignoring her bloody, dangling finger, the "dead woman" crawled over the robber's body, climbed out of the fresh grave, and headed for home. When she was found on the front porch, the family took her inside, mended her bloody hand, and delighted in her miraculous resurrection from the dead. Soon the local doctor arrived, and he announced that the woman had never been dead. Instead, she was a victim of a "coma," a new type of disease. After her sewn finger mended and she caught up on lost sleep, the woman resumed her role as wife and mother.

Meanwhile, her husband and the doctor visited the family cemetery to check out the woman's plot. There they found the unconscious body of the grave robber lying in the woman's coffin. When the husband tried to awaken the man, he discovered a lifeless body. The grave robber was dead—killed by his own knife that was sticking out of his back. Apparently, he had fallen on his weapon in the confusion of trying to escape from the vampirelike creature.

The legend states that the woman who had been brought back from the dead lived to a ripe old age and delighted county residents as she shared her personal experience quite often. Some believe that she had recognized her attackers, but never spoke their names and took their identities to her grave . . . the second and final time.

Central Maryland

THE COUNTIES OF HARFORD, BALTIMORE, HOWARD, CARROLL, AND Montgomery host some of the state's most captivating ghost tales and haunted sites. Of prominence is the legend of Black Aggie, known for generations as the region's most fearsome phantom; and many folks have heard of historic Ellicott City, where its ghost-walking tours attract both serious paranormal investigators and tourists interested in learning about local history—with a dab of fright. And who would guess that the basis for dreams-come-true lies beneath Montgomery County's busy streets.

Black Aggie

Mention famous Baltimore-area legends, and immediately longtime Maryland residents utter the name "Black Aggie." The words are often whispered to relay a sense of awe, respect, and, to a degree, fear. This might seem surprising, however, since the creature—with glowing red eyes that opened at midnight, and which was the subject of hundreds of tall tales and personal legends—was evicted and hauled away from its hometown more than forty years ago.

Our bizarre story begins at the turn of the twentieth century. That's when *Baltimore American* publisher Felix Agnus, a prominent citizen who had served as a Union general during the Civil

War, purchased an artwork to mark his family plot in Druid Ridge Cemetery, located in Pikesville, just outside the city limits. The eerie figure, installed at the graveyard atop a stone platform bearing the Agnus family name, was a knock-off reproduction of a piece of fine artwork that had been created by noted sculptor Augustus Saint-Gaudens. The original piece had been commissioned by historian Henry Adams, a descendant of the presidential Adams family; he was the grandson of the sixth U.S. president John Quincy Adams and great-grandson of Declaration of Independence signer and second U.S. president John Adams.

The original stunning, yet depressing, piece—unofficially named "Grief" by some observers—had been erected in Washington's Rock Creek Cemetery as a memorial to Henry Adams's wife Marian, who died while only in her forties. Apparently someone made an illegal casting of the original work, and publisher Agnus accepted a life-size imitation as the perfect figure to adorn his family plot and honor his deceased wife Annie Agnus. In 1907, the copy of the Saint-Gaudens creation was placed on its granite base outside Baltimore. Soon, a storm of controversy erupted over the appropriateness of owning and displaying the unsanctioned copy of the Washington-area sculpture.

Members of the Adams and Saint-Gaudens families protested the Agnus cemetery sculpted copy, and lawsuits were initiated. Saint-Gaudens's widow wanted the statue removed. Felix Agnus was adamant that his version of the monument remain at his Pikesville family plot. Agnus's argument against the suit was successful, and "Grief" remained solidly perched, all assumed, at the top of a rolling hillside among granite crosses, carved angels, and thousands of less distinctive stone markers.

Initially, Baltimore's Agnus memorial creature went unnoticed, but in the midst of the Roaring Twenties, for a reason we will never discover, the stone art piece seemed to develop a diabolical life of its own. It was shortly after Felix Agnus's death (on Halloween, October 31, 1925) that the legend was born. The contemplative and curious-looking creature seemed to awaken from its slumber and earned its very special name "Black Aggie."

For more than forty years, from the 1920s through the 1960s, the area surrounding the eerie metal creation became a must-visit site for daytime passersby and late evening adventurers. During

AGNUS

Sunday afternoons, slow-moving processions of automobiles bearing locals and tourists would drive the narrow lanes of Druid Ridge Cemetery, pausing to take Black Aggie photographs, which later were shown off to friends and neighbors. When darkness fell, however, less mannerly revelers arrived on foot, making secretive, unofficial pilgrimages to the "sinister" statue's site.

College fraternities decided Black Aggie would be an excellent assistant to evaluate applicants. As part of their initiation rites, hopefuls were ordered to sit in Black Aggie's lap to prove they were worthy of membership. One folktale claims that a young man died from a heart attack while in the statue's clutches, and the following morning workmen discovered the lifeless student's body beside Black Aggie's feet.

Naturally, more stories and tales combined to establish the statue's status as the region's premier urban legend. Some said that even walking beneath the creature's shadow would have dire consequences. Pregnant mothers claimed to experience miscarriages, and others told stories that no vegetation or flora would grow in the shade of Aggie's ominous figure. (Perhaps the latter was due to the constant traffic around the gravesite, destroying grass and plantings that had to be continually replaced.)

Many Baltimore-area family photo albums contain black-and-white pictures of children, teens, and adults posing beside Black Aggie, and some folks appear to be sitting in the monster's arms. Years ago, children would be afraid to even whisper the creature's name. They thought she would appear under the bed, come out, and scare them to death.

Those unsure of where exactly Black Aggie held court would have only to enter the cemetery and wait until the stoke of midnight, for it was at the bewitching hour when two bright red dots would appear. These were said to be the bristling fires of hell, glowing from the statue's demonic eyes.

As legends associated with Black Aggie grew more bizarre, visits by couples and groups were more numerous, and midnight escapades by crowds swelled in size and multiplied in frequency. Beneath the shrouded figure, young women lost their virginity, drunken parties were held, and wicked rituals were conducted. One story surfaced that in 1962 a workman found one of Black Aggie's arms, which had been cut off the night before. Another tale reported that the statue was the likeness of an area nurse, who was hanged in error for an unstated crime. Those responsible were said to have bought the statue as a penance to atone for their mistake and the accompanying guilt.

It will never be known how many fraternity initiates sat on Black Aggie's lap, felt the heat from her hands, and then jumped away at the last moment to avoid being crushed by the monster's grip. And we can only estimate the number of Baltimoreans who made unofficial pilgrimages to catch a glimpse of the eerie edifice in action. But there is no doubt that the numbers are substantial.

By the 1960s, vandalism from unauthorized nighttime visits and the legend's growing notoriety became serious disruptions to the operation, maintenance, and reputation of the peaceful, country-style cemetery. Eventually, the staff decided it could no longer handle the spell that Black Aggie had cast over multiple generations of Baltimore-area residents and thrill seekers. To help solve these growing problems, Agnus family descendants decided to remove the statue aptly named "Grief," which was causing much of the same for the cemetery staff.

Beau Reid is a lifelong area resident and family services counselor at Druid Ridge Cemetery, where the Agnus plot is located in the Annandale section, one of the oldest portions of the picturesque graveyard that opened in 1896. During an interview with him for the book *Baltimore Ghosts,* we stood together beside the empty pedestal at the monument where once the monster had reigned. Shaking his head, Reid said, "We get three or four calls a month about her, from people who want to come up and see where she used to be or to find out some information. We're constantly guiding people up here. They want to know the story and also ask how long she's been gone."

Reid said that if twenty or more people visit the cemetery for a service, several who happen to be in the forty-five- to sixty-year-old age range will mention Black Aggie and ask for directions to the Agnus grave. "Some very prominent citizens come up and share some of the high jinx they pulled years ago," Reid said, smiling. He added that he has seen pictures of people sitting proudly in Black Aggie's lap. "It's amazing, even though she's been gone a long time, people still make the trip to Druid Ridge, and people still share their stories about Black Aggie."

Thanks to very helpful and specific directions provided by Wayne Schaumburg, Baltimore historian and noted tour guide at Green Mount Cemetery, I caught up with Black Aggie—in Washington, D.C., only a block from the White House. In 1967, after she was hauled off her granite podium, Black Aggie was acquired (depending upon which source you discover) by the Maryland Institute of Art or the Smithsonian American Art Museum or the National Collection of Fine Arts or the National Museum of American Art. While she may have been displayed temporarily, most sources agree that for several years she was relegated to a dark corner beneath a stairwell in a museum basement.

In about 1987, the mystifying sculpture was transferred to the General Services Administration, which placed her on display in the courtyard of the Federal Judicial Center, located across from Lafayette Square, adjacent to the Dolley Madison House. Through a red-brick, gated archway, with a brass plate proclaiming "Entrance to 717 Madison Place," the Baltimore icon sits alone, beneath a street lamp and surrounded by shrubbery. Her veiled face gives the impression that she is asleep, inactive, and benign. Each day she is ignored, or at most glanced at, by federal workers who eat their lunch and chat casually at round picnic tables. Tourists carrying cameras and guide maps pass by, unfazed and unimpressed by the quiet, green-gray creature that seems to be asleep in the manicured garden.

None of the workers or visitors has any idea that in their midst sits a creature that had once achieved a horrifying celebrity status in her hometown. Who would have imagined that more than forty years since her departure from her Baltimore abode, just a passing mention of the words "Black Aggie" still has the power to delight, entertain, and, in some cases, even terrify?

John Wilkes Booth

American Revolutionary War officer Benedict Arnold was branded a traitor for making plans to surrender West Point, New York, to the British. Lee Harvey Oswald was labeled the infamous lone assassin of President John F. Kennedy in Dallas, Texas. John Wilkes Booth was tracked down and killed for shooting President Abraham Lincoln in Ford's Theatre in Washington, D.C.

These three names are among the most despised in American history, and the last—John Wilkes Booth—has earned a special place on the pedestals of infamy. His actions also tarnished his native state of Maryland, which was a hotbed of Southern sympathizers before, during, and after the Civil War. Booth was born in the northern part of the state, not far from the Pennsylvania border and Mason-Dixon Line. After shooting Lincoln, Booth hid in homes in the southern part of Maryland, before his eventual capture and death in northern Virginia

Certainly, incidents of hauntings—some involving the hated assassin—have been reported at the sites where Booth grew up, or where he killed the president and later stopped during his attempted escape. Those on the escape route include the Surratt House Museum in Clinton, Maryland, and the Dr. Samuel A. Mudd House Museum in Waldorf, Maryland. Over the years, strange tales also have been told about Tudor Hall, the former Booth estate in Harford County, where the family had lived for many years.

John Wilkes Booth was born in 1838 in Tudor Hall near the town of Bel Air. The country estate was the home where his father—British-born Shakespearian actor Junius Brutus Booth Sr.—had settled in the area in 1822. Junius and his wife Mary raised ten children at the home, including John Wilkes, whose actions in 1865 forever sullied the family name. It's said on hearing of Lincoln's assassination, John Wilkes's mother gathered all of her son's belongings, clothing, and photographs and burned them in the Tudor Hall fireplace. Apparently, the family decided that his crime was not bad enough to keep him out of the family burial plot.

To get the full story on the assassin's delivery and interment in his final resting place, I spoke to Wayne Schaumburg. A Baltimore native, historian, and schoolteacher, Wayne has been conducting popular graveyard tours for more than twenty years in Baltimore's Green Mount Cemetery, a sixty-eight-acre rectangular patch of earth located in the center of the historic town.

"This is the most asked-about grave in the cemetery," Wayne said, placing his hand against the tall, white obelisk bearing the family name BOOTH in block letters. "People get excited about it," he added, pointing to the infamous name of the assassin that is listed on the back of the tall stone.

Wayne explained that the name "John Wilkes," carved amidst several other members of his family, is the only indication that Abraham Lincoln's murderer is located in the Booth plot. ("Plot" as in area of ground, of course. One has to be careful to explain the precise meaning when using the words "Booth" and "plot" in the same sentence.)

But questions about how the murderer's corpse eventually arrived in Baltimore prompted Wayne to share a fascinating tale. The Booth family wanted their kin brought home. Wayne explained that in 1869, Edwin, an actor and John Wilkes's brother, arranged for the release of the assassin's body, which had been buried along with the other conspirators in the grounds of the Washington Penitentiary.

Edwin had no interest in turning the gravesite into a Confederate shrine or allowing the family plot to become a site that Union loyalists would desecrate. Therefore, there is no specific marker indicating precisely where John Wilkes is buried. The assassin's corpse arrived in Baltimore in February 1869. Because it was the middle of winter, the ground was too hard for the grave to be opened, so the body was stored in a holding vault at Green Mount until late June. It's written that the final ceremony was an eerie affair, held in the evening with lit torches used for illumination, and attended by Booth family members and a few friends. Smiling, Wayne told how a good deed backfired on a helpful clergyman who offered graveside comments at the assassin's service.

Since no religious person in the area was willing to speak at John Wilkes's requiem, the Booth family somehow engaged the spiritual talents of The Reverend Fleming James, an Episcopal minister from New York, who, some say, was visiting friends in the city. It is not known if the helpful reverend was informed that the deceased was the notorious murderer of the late, great president of the United States, or if the preacher assumed he was lending a helping hand to an average family in need. Nevertheless, when his congregation in New York discovered that their very own Reverend James had officiated at the ceremony of John Wilkes Booth, they dismissed the well-intentioned padre from his position as leader of their flock.

"There are stories," Wayne said, "that John Wilkes Booth is not really here, that he was never caught, and that he escaped to the Midwest and died at a very old age. Others say he was buried in

Virginia." Despite such rumors occasionally raising questions about whether the assassin's corpse actually rests in downtown Baltimore, the Booth plot continues to be the most visited and photographed site in Green Mount Cemetery.

Ghost of Peddler's Run

A familiar figure found throughout the villages in the American colonies was the traveling peddler. This distinctive and enterprising character offered a variety of wares from necessities, such as farming tools, sewing supplies, and cooking utensils, to more decorative items like silken materials and costume jewelry. He remained a familiar sight in rural towns and big-city neighborhoods until the first half of the twentieth century.

In the late 1700s in Harford County, north of the present-day Conowingo Dam, the ghost of a restless, headless peddler began to haunt the area along the banks of the Susquehanna River. And while the cause of the haunting was eventually put to rest, the tale continues to be told in the area originally named Rock Run, but more appropriately changed to Peddler's Run.

In 1763, John, the owner of a gristmill at Rock Run, was heading toward his mill when he noticed a slumped body near the path. When he reached the lifeless figure, he discovered that it was missing its head. The deadly wound appeared to be a clean cut, but the head was nowhere in the vicinity. The miller organized a quick burial party and disposed of the stranger in a plain box near the site where the body was discovered.

Word spread through the community about the murder, and it wasn't long before a peddler's walking stick and sack were found. These items caused people to recall that two peddlers had been seen in the area. One wore a menacing-looking sword on his belt. Area folks surmised that there probably had been a falling out and the sword bearer had decapitated his associate, then fled the region, leaving his former traveling companion along the trail. Certainly there was no way to arrest and try anyone for the crime, so the case was essentially closed.

About a half year later, one early evening as John was heading toward home from his mill, he saw a strange figure standing near the grave of the murdered peddler. The visitor seemed to be bending over and poking at the ground with the end of a strong stick. It was the type carried by all peddlers to support their pack, and it also was handy to shake at attacking stray dogs.

As John approached closer, the stranger stood erect and the miller noticed the figure had no head. As the miller screamed, the headless man ran into the nearby marshland, stabbing the small end of his stick into the ground along his way. Soon other residents admitted seeing the headless man along the same trail. Many said he had done the same thing, poked the ground with his stick before disappearing into the nearby marsh. With folks in those days being heavily superstitious and afraid of the walking dead, they avoided going near the area where the headless roamer had been reported. This lack of traffic affected John's business, causing him to close his mill.

In a *Baltimore Sun* story about this legend, printed in 1954, writer John T. Starr noted, "The mill fell into disrepair and the path along the mill-race grew up in weeds. No one knew whether the ghost still performed his strange antics for no one came his way."

It wasn't until eighty years after the murder, in 1843, that a farmer named Joseph was digging a drainage ditch near the old mill on the property he had bought and uncovered a human skull. Apparently, the headless peddler's missing noggin had been found at last. Knowing the old headless peddler ghost tale, Joseph located the murdered peddler's grave, reunited the skull with the original skeleton, and reburied the murdered nameless soul.

Starr offered a solution to the headless man's antics, explaining that "His strange motions of poking at the grave with a long stick . . . and running to the swamp to poke at the spot where the head reposed was simply to tell the passerby of his headless plight and how it could be rectified. When the head was united with the remains of the rest of the body, the spirit of the peddler rested in peace."

In a later *Baltimore* Sun story, John Sherwood wrote, "But even today, 'careful people' pick up their steps when they pass this spot. A new road was constructed as the original path was abandoned because of the legend."

Suspended Sailor

There's an unusual story associated with a sailor's grave in Spesutia Church Cemetery of St. George's Episcopal Parish in Perryman, Maryland—located off U.S. Route 40, east of Baltimore between Edgewood and Aberdeen. Some think this story is the most unusual graveyard tale they have ever heard. See what you think.

John Clark Monk was a sailor, an adventurer, and, certainly, a bit eccentric. In his will, the seaman demanded that since he had spent so much time sailing the Seven Seas, upon his death his body should never touch the earth. According to the legend, when he died at sea, per his instructions, Mr. Monk was "pickled" in a barrel of rum, or some other alcoholic or preservative substance, and his body found its way to the Harford County graveyard. There the remains were placed in a lead shroud and the encased body was deposited in the grave pit, but suspended by chains or lead straps, so his remains will never touch the earth.

Visitors to the traditional-looking, coffinlike marble marker of John Clark Monk can peek into the grave by taking a flashlight and peering between the wide gaps in the dark stones that hold up Monk's large, boxlike, aboveground tomb. Those with a keen eye and a fair degree of patience can see the outline of the straps, leading toward the center of the gravesite. There the persistent grave hunter will get a glimpse of the lead shroud that is said to hold the remains of a rather eccentric sailor, who provided us with a marvelous tidbit of unusual boneyard lore.

Haunted Covered Bridge

Jericho, Gunpowder Falls, Jerusalem Mill—the names alone conjure up images of mysterious activity, battle scenes, and events of biblical proportion. Put them all together and you tend to believe that this eastern portion of Maryland where all three converge has a good chance of being haunted.

Such might be the case at Jericho Covered Bridge, located on Jericho Road as it crosses from Baltimore County to Harford County. The wooden structure is close to Jerusalem Mill, a 235-year-old stone structure on the banks of the Little Gunpowder Falls River. Along with the nearby village, the mill is listed on the National Register of Historic Places. The covered bridge, about eighty-eight feet long and fifteen feet wide, is located along a narrow, wooded rural road, and it is the last such historic bridge in both counties. Built in the mid-1800s, this enclosed, wooden-truss bridge has witnessed its share of local and national history. Like other covered bridges that once were prevalent across the country, the Jericho Bridge helped travelers, animals, and wagons pass over the rolling waterway. It also speeded up the transport of flour from the nearby mill to waiting merchants.

No one knows when the ghost tales began, but along with haunted houses and old inns and cemeteries, covered bridges have attracted the attention of storytellers, historians, and ghost hunters. In addition to several books about haunted covered bridges, a number of websites encourage viewers to share their experiences. Often these comments relate to nighttime explorations, when ghosters (my term for ghost hunters) try to capture photographs of apparitions or evidence of possible spirit energy.

A few legends have seemed to latch onto the aging timbers of Jericho Covered Bridge. One tale mentions sightings of slaves that were hanged from the rafters of the bridge, apparently while trying to escape across the Mason-Dixon Line into nearby Pennsylvania, which was a free state during the Civil War. Because many Marylanders were sympathetic to the Southern cause, there was a strong presence of slave kidnappers and nightriders, who would grab up free blacks and sell them back into slavery. Could escaping slaves have been hanged from the bridge? Possibly—except that some sources state the bridge was built in 1865, at the end of the Civil War. Others sources estimate the building date as between 1850 and 1865.

Ghost hunters have reported capturing orbs—round globelike images that they believe indicate the presence of spirit energy—in some bridge photos. Other people claim their cars have stopped unexplainably inside the covered bridge. And one daytime tourist reported seeing women in old-fashioned clothing along the roadway and a nearby stream. However, when the visitor turned back to view the location of the sighting, the images had seemed to disappear.

The nearby historic village of Jerusalem Mill is known for its living-history demonstrations, such as blacksmithing, leather working, open-hearth cooking, and candle making. On certain week-ends, visiting reenactors pose as hunters, explorers, and traders from the Colonial period. One wonders: Are the reported sightings nothing but historic reenactors who may have strayed a bit beyond the village boundaries—or something else?

Patapsco Female Institute

Abandoned schools, hospitals, and military sites are among the best locations favored by ghost hunters, paranormal researchers, and weekend adventurers. Those who dare to check out local haunted locations are sometimes referred to as "legend trippers."

Patapsco Female Institute is one place you'll find these folks. Near Ellicott City are the decaying remains of this former girls school that opened in 1839. With its Greek Revival architecture featuring tall columns and yellow granite stonework, in its heyday it resembled the classic plantation homes of the rich and famous of America's Southern society, to which many of its resident students belonged.

According to Troy Taylor in his book *The Haunting of America,* conditions at the school were much less pleasant than the young ladies had been accustomed to at home. Unsatisfactory sanitary conditions and poor heating caused outbreaks of influenza and croup, which contributed to the deaths of several students.

Taylor related the tale of one pneumonia victim named Annie, the daughter of a rich Southern planter who let it be known that she was unhappy at the school. Soon after arriving, she wrote home, protesting her "incarceration" and displeasure with the educational institution's isolated rural location near a quiet mill town. Unfortunately, Annie died during her first winter at the school, and her restless ghost—wearing a long gown—is believed to roam the abandoned complex, apparently still annoyed with her family, which indirectly caused her early death so far from home.

After the Civil War, the school's attendance began to decline, and it closed in 1891. Subsequent owners used it as a private residence and a hotel; in 1917, the former school became a hospital for wounded soldiers serving in World War I. "It is unknown," Taylor wrote, "just how many soldiers may have passed away in the old building, but one has to wonder if any of them chose to stay behind in the massive building as time passed on."

After the 1940s, its last occupants left. Today, the historic site is known as the Patapsco Female Institute Historic Park, part of the Mt. Ida Visitor Center in Ellicott City. The ruins of the old school continue to be a magnet for ghost investigators, who take photographs searching for evidence of spirit energy.

Ellicott City Mansions

In what was once farmland and forests west of Baltimore stands Ellicott City, established as a mill town in the late 1700s. As years passed, the small village became a manufacturing center, and in 1831, it was the site of America's first railroad terminal. With a bustling economy, a rural setting not far from Maryland's largest seaport city of Baltimore, and ample land upon which to grow crops and establish estates, many impressive homes and manors sprang up in this locale on the eastern edge of Howard County.

Over the years, stories have survived of ghostly activity in several of the area's homes and businesses, enough tales to maintain interest in a wonderful ghost tour in the heart of the town. Thanks to my friend Troy Taylor, nationally recognized speaker and author of dozens of ghost books, the following stories have been summarized from his book, *Haunting of America*.

Lilburn Hall

Lilburn Hall, an impressive residence built in 1857, is home of our first ghost tale that some attribute to several tragedies that occurred to the family of Henry Richard Hazelhurst, the prosperous builder who made a fortune trading in iron during the Civil War. The builder lost his wife and several children suddenly; one daughter is believed to have died while giving birth at Lilburn. Outliving most of his family, Hazelhurst died alone at the home at the age of eighty-five.

It wasn't until another family purchased and moved into the home that the stories began. Footsteps were heard in the tower, and other unexplained sounds occurred. After a Christmas fire almost turned deadly and destroyed much of the mansion, the owners rebuilt the home, but they replaced the Gothic-style peaks with stone, giving it a fortress appearance.

The house was again sold in the 1960s, and the new owners heard phantom footsteps; also their family dog avoided entering a second-floor room. A chandelier began swaying during a party and frightened the guests. Windows in the tower seem to open on their own, and servants have reported hearing a child's cries and smelling cigar smoke in the empty library. One housekeeper claimed to have seen various apparitions, including a man and a little girl.

Some believe the architectural change after the Christmas fire was not appreciated by the original builder and is the source of the ghostly activity. Others say the unseen wanderer might be the daughter who died in the home while giving birth.

Ghost of Mt. Ida

The mansion known as Mt. Ida was designed in the early 1800s, and it is one of the most prominent landmarks of the town. It was built for William Ellicott, grandson of one of the founders of Ellicott Mills. William died at the age of forty-three, unable to enjoy his new home. In the 1850s, a judge and his family moved in, and descendants lived there until the 1970s. According to author Taylor, it is with this family that the ghosts are associated.

After the judge's death, the house was left to his children. His son died in a boating accident, and his three maiden sisters all lived in the house until they died. The last to pass on was Miss Ida, whom many believe is the mansion's most prominent ghost.

According to residents and workers, they have heard the sounds of keys rattling as Miss Ida roams her domain. While living, this last family resident would carry a ring of keys at all times.

Oak Lawn's Cooking Ghost

Oak Lawn, also called Hayden House, was a small stone dwelling built in 1842. The original owner, the county's first clerk, lived there with his wife and six children until his death in 1850.

Over the years the structure has been used by many municipal agencies, including the board of education and district court. Today it is home of the Howard County Circuit Court. In the 1970s, while occupied by the county office of parole and probation, staff reported strange events. Lights would turn on and off by themselves; a coffee pot would heat up, even when unplugged; an unoccupied chair would rock on its own; and unexplained footsteps were heard. One employee reported seeing the apparition of an unidentified man, but no one was discovered after a search of the building.

There also were smells of soup or bacon and eggs that could be noticed throughout the building, day and night. When no source of the simmering food could be found, the frustrated searchers dubbed the phantom the "cooking ghost."

One employee claimed to have seen several strange occurrences, including cloth napkins being folded by themselves and also a mist-like, hazy ball of vapor that vanished from view in the building.

Melody Simmons, a Howard County bureau reporter for the *Evening Sun,* wrote about the building's ghosts in an article published on Halloween Day 1980. Under the headline "Alleged Ghost Spooks Workers at Courthouse," her story adds other details to the legend. Employees have reported smells of apple cobbler and bacon, apparently the phantom's favorites. Other workers noted that the unseen ghost has called out to various staff members using their proper names. Many suggest that the permanent invisible resident is the ghost of Edwin Parsons Hayden, the attorney who built the home and lived there until a tragic death, at the age of thirty-eight.

While some people may think the idea of a resident ghost would help relieve the dull routines of the average workday, the mysterious presence has some drawbacks. "Many employees refuse to work nights in the courthouse," Simmons wrote, "leaving the building at the 4:30 P.M. closing time. 'I'm just too scared,' one clerk says. 'When I do work at night, I like to have someone sitting in here with me at all times. And I am even afraid to walk upstairs to the bathroom alone.'"

Today the old building is still in use as the Howard County Circuit Court. When asked if the old building is still haunted, the staff person on the other end of the phone paused and said, "Well. That depends . . ."

"On whom you ask?" I added, trying to break the uncomfortable silence.

And in a relieved voice, the staffer replied, "That's correct."

The Red Light

Ghosts of murdered slaves haunt the riverbanks of the Susquehanna River, north of the Conowingo Dam, in both Cecil and Harford counties. The Mason-Dixon Line runs east and west, separating Maryland and Pennsylvania, only a short distance north of present-day U.S. Route 1 in that northern section of Maryland. The boundary divided the Northern and Southern states during the Civil War. Even today, people recognize that centuries-old demarcation drawn in the 1760s by Charles Mason and Jeremiah Dixon.

During the War Between the States, slaves traveling along the Underground Railroad followed the North Star, heading for freedom. One of their first objectives was to reach the state of Pennsylvania. Secret trails throughout the Delmarva Peninsula were heavily traveled escape routes leading through Wilmington, Delaware, to Philadelphia, Pennsylvania. These two cities were home to many abolitionists, who were eager to help any slave that made it that far.

Other runaways avoided these more populated areas. Instead, they moved through the marshes and guts along the western side of the Delmarva Peninsula, following the woods and winding banks along the Susquehanna River. No one knows how many "fugitives" arrived in the Promised Land of Pennsylvania. But many never crossed the line because they were killed or captured by slave kidnappers and Southern sympathizers. These nightriders were on the lookout for fugitives, for after being captured they could be sold back into slavery.

Other terrified slaves, who managed to avoid capture, died from exposure to the elements, some freezing to death during a harsh winter. Still more succumbed to animal attacks, and disease. Their remains rest where they died, in unmarked, unnoticed, and forgotten graves in the ground of Maryland's Eastern Shore and western counties.

One story persists, however, about a family of slaves heading north along the mighty Susquehanna River. They were on a makeshift raft, sailing at night so the darkness would help conceal their flight from spies and bounty hunters. The frightened fugitives worked together, straining on their oars against the waters that were rushing down the rocky rapids at Smith's Falls.

A red light was their objective. They had been told that a red-colored lantern would mark the safe landing place. The signal would be expected to appear on either side of the river in the county of Harford or Cecil, depending upon which area was safest on that particular night. When they made it to shore, the slaves would be given shelter and food; but most of all, they would meet those who would lead them to a safe station house. There they would be able to rest, regroup, and head further north to freedom. Their primary goal was to travel out of the long reach of their masters and others interested in claiming them as a prize to be bound, gagged, and delivered like property to be traded in for hard cash. But on this night, things did not go as planned.

The red light burned, the signal was given, and the raft carrying anticipation, fear, and hope made it safely to shore. But the faces surrounding the brightly lit campfire were not friendly. Slave hunters had gotten word of the plan, had taken the abolitionists' place, and waited for the human cargo to arrive. No one recorded what occurred when the frightened blacks met the unfriendly whites, but it's not hard to imagine. Some say the new arrivals resisted and were killed and then tossed into the nearby river or covered in a shallow, unmarked grave. Others, however, believe the slave hunters spared their lives, for the captives were worth much more alive and worth nothing dead. The kidnappers redeemed their captives for cash and congratulated themselves on a profitable evening's outing. In either case, the slaves' long road to freedom ended that night at the solitary red light on the banks of the Susquehanna River.

Some people claim they've heard the moans of the raft of doomed slaves. There also are reports of sightings, through the gray mist over the water, of floating bodies that disappear as the sun burns off the surface fog. And at night, fishermen, hikers, and boaters say they've seen an unexplained red ghost light, which appears in the forests just above the Susquehanna shoreline.

Gold in the Ground

Montgomery County is one of the state's most populous, congested, and historic; and with its proximity to Washington, D.C., it has a fair number of ghost tales. You can take your pick of historic sites with reports of specters in old mansions, such as Clara Barton's old house, and the Montgomery County Historical Society is well known for conducting its popular ghost tours with horror and history related to murder, disease, and thwarted love. There are even reports of mysterious happenings at Chestnut Lodge Hospital (or Sanitarium or Asylum, depending upon the source of the story). But very few Maryland and East Coast locations can boast a legacy of gold mining that occurred right below today's interstates and commercial and residential districts. And even today, some dreamers head to the streams and rivers, only a few miles from the White House, to pan for the world's most valuable and glittering substance.

The first reports of gold in Montgomery County surfaced in 1849 on Samuel Ellicott's farm near Brookville. In 1861, a Union soldier from the 71st Pennsylvania Regiment was stationed outside of Washington, D.C., near Great Falls. It's said he discovered gold while washing dishes in a stream, and in 1867 the first shaft was sunk, establishing the Maryland Mine, located near the intersection of Falls Road and MacArthur Boulevard.

Gold mining and panning continued, with a half-dozen operations at work in 1901. Commercial exploration and production ambled along until a few years after World War II, when it ended about 1950. But according to the Maryland Geological Survey, nearly two dozen mining operations were active at some time in Montgomery County alone, many along Falls Road between I-270 and River Road. While no great finds comparable to those in the Wild West were discovered, there were reports of some good-size nuggets being taken from the area of Great Falls. Due to the increase in the price of gold, panning-style prospecting continues, with a small number of hopeful hobbyists and treasure hunters still seeking both fortune and fun through gold mining.

But where history ends, folklore and legend begin. Old mine shafts can be discovered by accident, and some curious explorers have spent their time seeking them out. However, most are on private property and forbidden to enter, and state and federal land also requires permission to access and explore. Since they have been abandoned for so long, these closed mining operations are dangerous, and personal injury is a more likely outcome than riches. Remnants of the Great Falls operations that have been fenced off to restrict public access include the old Ford Mine, which collapsed in 1890, and several shafts of the old Maryland Mine, one reaching a depth of more than two hundred feet.

But some suggest there is more under the busy urban highways than empty, water-filled caverns. Some believe Montgomery County's old gold mines hold the bodies of ghostly miners who had been trapped in cave-ins or lost in the tunnels and never returned to the surface.

From the Maryland Ghost and Spirit Association website, another rather interesting anecdote is worth sharing. In 1918, while a mining company was digging tunnels and ditches, searching for gold outside Washington, D.C., rumors circulated that these trenches actually were preparations for a German attack on the federal government and its headquarters located in the nearby nation's capital.

Opera House Ghost

Westminster, the county seat of Carroll County, is home to a fair number of restless spirits—so many that the Carroll County Public Library presents a guided ghost tour in the historic town each October. Among the event's most popular ghost tales is one told beside the Main Street Opera House, which was the site of a murder in the years following the Civil War.

According to the legend, while presenting his singing and comic act on stage, Marshall Buell, a traveling entertainer from the Deep South, had apparently annoyed several rowdy members of the small-town audience. After the program, as the minstrel was preparing to leave town and travel to his next engagement, he was attacked and murdered in an alley behind the building. His lifeless body was discovered the next morning, and soon afterwards reports of a phantomlike figure, dressed in the attire of the murdered entertainer, spread throughout the area. Of course, the legend is passed down each year to those taking the nighttime haunted tour, and participants have reported seeing the shadowy image of Marshall Buell—who some suggest may have told one joke too many.

Baltimore

As Maryland's largest city and the birthplace of our national anthem, Baltimore is known as one of the country's most haunted towns. Edgar Allan Poe, John Wilkes Booth, grave robbers, and Civil War soldiers and sailors all have left their spirited signatures in cemeteries, forts, and historic neighborhoods throughout the town.

'Oh Say Can You See!'

Are there ghosts at Fort McHenry? It seems a number of people think so, including folks who spend a lot of time at the forty-three-acre national monument and historic shrine, primarily known as the birthplace of our country's national anthem.

In a 2004 interview for the book *Baltimore Ghosts: History, Mystery, Legends and Lore,* Park Ranger Vince Vaise, a Baltimore native, said, "We have a number of ghost tales associated with Fort McHenry. And while we don't want to be known as a haunted fort, there's a point where the ghost stories and the folklore become a part of history."

Over the years—through documentaries, such as the History Channel's *Haunted Baltimore,* and numerous newspaper and magazine articles, including an autumn 1986 issue of *National Parks* magazine—tales of unusual events at the Baltimore fortification have been reported. Before we begin the ghost tales, and there are several to share, it's important to understand Fort McHenry's significance and the role it played in our country's history.

Francis Scott Key, a Baltimore lawyer, witnessed the twenty-five-hour enemy bombardment of the city from the deck of a British ship on September 12 and 13, 1814. During the attack—when the British fleet fired nearly eighteen hundred shells at the fort—the mammoth thirty- by forty-two-foot flag made by Mary Pickersgill remained flying high for all to see. Key was so inspired by the sight that he began writing the stirring poem that would serve as the words to our national anthem.

Like the British fleet, the Crown's attacking land forces, when met with extensive entrenchments on the outskirts of Baltimore, decided to withdraw. On September 15, the frustrated attackers retreated and sailed south through the Chesapeake Bay.

While Fort McHenry would never experience another attack, it remained active as a political and military prison during the Civil War. During the latter years of World War I and afterwards, a three thousand-bed army hospital was located around the fort. If it's true that tragedy, death, and sudden unfortunate events contribute to the presence of ghosts, Fort McHenry has good reason to be haunted.

During the British bombardment on September 13, 1814, an incoming bomb exploded on the gun emplacement at Bastion 3. The direct hit killed members of the Maryland militia, including an officer named Lieutenant Levi Clagett. Some people think his spirit appears at that site and also walks along the ramparts. Also referred to as "Clagett's Bastion," the location is one of the five points that juts out from the star-shaped fort. Visitors and employees have reported sighting a soldier, wearing a uniform appropriate to the 1814 era, walking in that area. A natural reaction to the sighting is to think that the figure in uniform is an actor or reenactor. However, when informed that there were no performers in costume on the grounds on that particular day, the visitors who reported the sightings were more than a little surprised.

Years ago, park staff that worked in a two-story building inside the fortification, which for years served as an enlisted men's barracks, claimed to see a figure dressed in white walking on the building's second floor. They also reported hearing heavy footsteps, being disturbed by doors and windows either slammed shut or left open, and finding furniture moved out of place. There have been reports of a woman looking out from a second-floor window and of hearing footsteps on the porch of the enlisted soldiers' quarters that are located inside the walls of the fort.

A Maryland artist was in the old buildings reviewing some historical documents. As he walked through a small doorway that required him to duck, he said, "I got hit like I was struck with a frying pan. It was while I was going through the doorframe. I mean, I was out cold. I was gone, out like a light."

The artist said he knew at the time that he had not simply bumped his head against the top of the frame or accidentally tapped into a low beam. When the park ranger escort returned, he told the artist he was surprised at the force of the attack, but did not seem surprised that an unusual event had occurred.

"That's our resident ghost," the ranger told the dazed visitor, and then the park worker shared his own story about being pushed down the stairs by a woman dressed in early-nineteenth-century clothing.

It's been suggested that the ghost had been a sergeant's wife, and that her husband and two children had died from a plague or epidemic that occurred in Baltimore during the 1820s.

Recalling his personal attack experience, the artist said, "I had no cuts, no bruises, no lumps, no nothing. But it was powerful. I hit my knees, and I was face first down on the floor. I attribute it to the lady ghost."

Perhaps the fort's most often told haunted tale involves the restless spirit of twenty-eight-year-old Private John Drew, who had been assigned to guard duty along the fort's outer battery on November 14, 1880. Unfortunately, the young soldier was discovered in the morning asleep at his post. Drew was ordered to a cell in the guard house, which is located in the entrance building. Embarrassed at failing in his duty and at being arrested, as well as upset that his army career was over and his comrades would never give him any respect, Drew smuggled a musket into his cell. Soon after locking the prisoner up, the guards heard a shot from the area of Drew's confinement. When they unlocked the barred metal door, they found that Drew had placed the muzzle of the weapon in his mouth and had used his toe to pull the trigger.

Visitors claim they have felt a distinct chill in the cell where Drew took his life. Others say they have sighted a figure—dressed in a long watch coat or cape and wearing a military-style cap—walking the same outer battery where the young soldier had been assigned more than 120 years ago.

Most park staff members seem to agree that the intense interest in ghosts at Fort McHenry was a direct result of a series of Halloween events that were conducted several decades ago. Although these ghost tours were popular, the park administrators did not want the historic shrine to be labeled "the haunted fort," and therefore discontinued them. Instead, they said the emphasis should be on the hallowed site's significant role in America's history.

While the ghost tours are no longer held, interest in Fort McHenry's phantoms seems to persist. Perhaps this is because of John Drew, Levi Clagett, and other unnamed specters who continue to be sighted and have their presences felt at the birthplace of "The Star-Spangled Banner."

USS Constellation

In the shadows of Baltimore's modern skyline sits a wooden relic of times long past. To some, it offers a hint of history; to others she suggests a sense of mystery. It's the USS *Constellation*, one of the city's most haunted sites. To understand the story, one should know there were two wooden-hulled vessels christened USS *Constellation*. The first was a frigate built in Baltimore and launched in 1797; it battled French ships and privateers. After the War of 1812, it sailed into the Mediterranean Sea to fight the Barbary Coast pirates. In the 1820s and 1830s, the frigate interdicted slave ships trying to enter the United States with their human cargo. This original ship, the U.S. frigate *Constellation*, was in active service until 1845, and it was scrapped in 1853. Among her commanders was Captain Thomas Truxtun, who directed the *Constellation*'s battle against the French ships *L'Insurgente* and *La Vengeance*.

The second *Constellation*, now in Baltimore's Inner Harbor, is a sloop-of-war that was launched in 1855, only a few years before the outbreak of the Civil War. It patrolled off the mouth of the Congo River, looking for ships participating in the illegal slave trade, capturing three slave ships and freeing 705 captives. With the outbreak of the Civil War it protected American commerce from Confederate raiders. Following the War Between the States, the USS *Constella-*

tion served in a number of roles, including years as a training ship for midshipmen at the U.S. Naval Academy at Annapolis, Maryland. During the subsequent decades, the ship was used primarily for training and ceremonial purposes.

But since the mid-1950s, it has had a visible presence in the city of Baltimore, where it was made accessible to Inner Harbor tourists in the 1970s. And soon there were tales about ghosts roaming over, under, around, and through the vessel's decks. Much of this talk is because ghost stories and legends seem to be automatically attached to old ships, and the USS *Constellation* is about as old as you can get.

Reports of paranormal sightings on Baltimore's floating museum have been printed in newspapers and magazines and also featured on the History Channel documentary *Haunted Baltimore.* In the book *Baltimore Ghosts,* Kennedy Hickman, at that time curator and historian for the USS *Constellation* Museum, said if there are any ghosts aboard, these spirits seem to be roaming a ship other than the one on which they had served, for the current vessel is believed to have very little material used in its construction from the original Baltimore-built frigate. Nevertheless, three stories seem to be the most popular and repeated, and they all are associated with the first vessel. They include tales of Neil Harvey, Captain Truxtun, and a young boy who died on a lower deck.

During an engagement in 1799, while the ship was in a battle against the French ship *La Vengeance,* Neil Harvey supposedly ran from his post. This was a serious offense, and there are several suggested endings to Harvey's maritime career. The sailor was hanged, or he was run through with a sword, or he was strapped to the front of a cannon and then blown apart. In the twentieth century, the ghostly figure of Neil Harvey—with his limbs all found and replaced in the correct locations—had been reported floating across the decks of the ship.

Commander Thomas Truxtun is said to be the ship's second resident ghost. Congress presented the frigate's late-eighteenth-century captain a medal for his excellent command of the *Constellation* during battles against the French in 1799 and 1800. But in modern times, the old salt seems to enjoy giving guided tours of the ship. In 1964, late one afternoon, a Catholic priest was leaving the ship and passed a few staff members who were closing up the museum. The reverend paused to compliment the staff on the fine presentation he had just received from a costumed guide on one of the lower decks. The staff members, who knew they had no inter-preter working on the vessel at that time, went aboard and inspected the entire ship. They found no one else, in or out of a late-eighteenth-century naval uniform, on board.

Young boys served on sailing ships as messengers, cook's helpers, officer's aides, ammunition carriers, and sick bay atten-dants. It's said one small boy, who served on the ship in the 1820s, was killed below decks. There is no reason given. It could have been an accident, a game or prank gone awry, or even a murder or beating. Nevertheless, there have been reports of a boy phantom appearing to visitors at various times.

In 1955, the *Baltimore Sun* ran a blurred photograph of a naval officer marching across the deck of the ship. The photo was report-edly taken by a U.S. Navy officer who had set up his camera on a tripod on the top deck. The story states, "At 11:59 P.M., to be exact, the Navy officer 'detected a faint scent in the air—a certain some-thing not unlike gunpowder.'" After his eerie picture appeared in the daily newspaper, the common-held belief that the ship was haunted was reinforced a hundred-fold.

When asked about the presence of ghosts on board, and it is a question posed quite often, Ken replied, "We try to politely debunk the stories." However, he referred to one tale quite different from the legends. It has a historical link, and it is one that even the cura-tor and other staff members find fascinating—and maybe even believable.

The account involves an entry in the *Diary of Yeoman Moses Saf-ford, USS Constellation*, 1862–1865. The statement about a paranor-mal incident is dated June 20, 1863, when Moses Safford, a lawyer from Kittery, Maine, was the ranking staff petty officer. Summariz-ing the entry, it states that Ike Simmons, a cook's mate who was in the brig, reported that two seamen—who had died recently on board—appeared before him dancing and singing. After noting that these reports were having a troubling effect upon the rest of the crew, the log stated: "Twice on stormy nights last fall, Campbell, the captain of the forecastle, whom we lost in the Atlantic (in 1862), was supposed to have been seen standing near the lee cathead.

Whatever may be the explanation of these phenomena, the sentences which Simmons has received will tend to discourage the men from giving undue publicity to their supernatural observations."

During recent times, a few of the staff workers in the *Constellation*'s offices and gift shop area have reported unusual occurrences. More than once, the figure of a man has been seen in the gift shop, after hours, wandering among the aisles. And then he suddenly disappears. Books have fallen off the shelves without any logical cause.

Why would ghost sailors who had served on the original frigate that was scrapped and destroyed decide to haunt a different vessel with the same name? Perhaps they are in search of a maritime home that is similar to the one on which they spent so much time. Maybe they don't realize their earthly existence is over. Whoever offers an explanation is providing nothing more than a guess.

But based on the account in Safford's diary, the sloop-of-war *Constellation*'s more believable spirits may be dancing below decks to a mysterious tune that modern mortal ears are unable to hear.

Phantom of the Heights

There were mysterious sightings on the east side of Baltimore in the summer of 1951, and after more than a half century has passed, the strange events associated with "the phantom" remain unsolved. Some have suggested the neighborhood bedlam was a mini version of the panic about a dozen years earlier in New Jersey, during the Orson Welles broadcast of *War of the Worlds*. Even though the comparison is a bit exaggerated, for those who lived near the O'Donnell Heights neighborhood, the terror was just as real.

For several weeks, residents of the row-house neighborhood claimed a strange presence was terrorizing their community. The object of concern was not your run-of-the-mill basic burglar or prowler. Instead, this "phantom," as it was named, possessed supernatural powers that allowed it to leap with apparent ease from twenty-foot-tall buildings and jump over six-foot-high, barb-wire-topped cemetery fences.

The fiend was described as wearing black robes and lurking at night in search of its prey. Break-ins, family disturbances, teenager mischief, and just about anything out of the ordinary was attributed to the phantom.

In a July 25, 1951, article in the *Sun*, the reporter shared comments from the dozen residents he had interviewed. His front-page article captured the attention of readers throughout the city. The writer reported a situation at midnight, when "throughout the project people waited—in nervous groups on porches and behind drawn shades—for the phantom to strike." One man kept lookout, while resting atop a garbage can, with his .12-gauge shotgun for protection. Other weapons held at the ready included pipes, clubs, baseball bats, and butcher knives.

A woman complained that her husband, who had been on watch so many nights for the creature, was suffering because his "eyeballs ache from staying awake so long." Another man announced that after the black-cape-clad phantom had jumped off a roof, he and friends "chased him down into the graveyard." Many folks believed the phantom dwelled in one of the old graveyards surrounding the community. There are frequent reports of residents chasing the phantom up "Cemetery Hill" and "Graveyard Hill." There was a claim that the phantom was seen "under that big sarcophagus," and one resident swore the creature "went back to his grave."

Several cemeteries—including Mount Carmel Cemetery, Oheb Shalom Cemetery, the German Cemetery *Gottesacker, Der Ersted* ("The First God's Field"), and St. Stanislaus Cemetery—surround the community, and all of the boneyards are within an easy leap and bound for the phantom.

Eventually, every barking dog and mischievous incident was blamed on the elusive wraith. Police on patrol began arresting youngsters who were hiding in graveyards, and the youths blamed the lure of the phantom for their actions. Also, other youngsters from distant sections of the city were patrolling the heights' streets, attempting to snare the specter and make the news.

No one knows who or what the O'Donnell Heights Phantom was, or where the black-robed wraith went, for it vanished as mysteriously as it had arrived, and the mystery of the summer of 1951 remains unsolved.

Master of Horror

Edgar Allan Poe—the mere mention of the one-syllable surname "Poe" conjures up images associated with a dark and solitary bird, cloaked figures, penetrating eyes, thumping hearts beating beneath floorboards, and wailing sounds escaping walled-up tombs. Today, so many years after his death in Baltimore in 1849, people are still curious about the mysterious circumstances surrounding the event.

Many cities claim the literary icon as their own. Poe homes and monuments are located in New York, Philadelphia, and Richmond, all places where he lived and worked. The University of Virginia, where the famous writer attended classes, boasts of its "Raven Society." But Baltimore—site of the scribe's home and, more importantly, city of the author's death and grave—lays rightful claim to the most permanent association with America's first master of horror.

There can be little argument that Baltimore nurtures its association with the famous writer, sponsoring an annual Poe Festival, offering tours of the Poe House, and holding documents and memorabilia at the Poe Society. But the most fascinating and captivating custom involves the "Poe Toaster." Upon first hearing the term, most people immediately imagine a special type of appliance, but the nearly six-decade custom has nothing to do with heating bread before dashing off to work. Here is a summary of the Charm City ritual.

In the center of downtown Baltimore—under cover of darkness and with a cloak of mystery quite befitting the ritual's deceased recipient—one of the most unusual and long-continuing modern customs occurs. This event centers around an individual called the "Poe Toaster." No one knows his identity, age, occupation, or why he began the unusual practice in the earliest hours of January 19, 1949—on the one-hundredth anniversary of Edgar's death. But each year between midnight and 6 A.M., this unidentified caller returns and enters Westminster Cemetery.

His visit is short and with a solitary purpose: to pay tribute to the writer by leaving distinctive calling cards—three red roses and a partially filled bottle of cognac—at the base of Poe's grave. As the hours pass toward the late evening of January 18, and time passes into the following day's early morning hours, small clusters of visitors take up lookout posts along the street corners surrounding the graveyard. Some sit in cars, with heaters running. Others walk the cold city streets, wrapped in blankets and wearing heavy, overstuffed coats to ward off the icy winds and frosty morning chill. A few even sit in portable folding chairs, handy binoculars resting on the puffy quilts that surround their freezing bodies. They're all awaiting the annual appearance of the Toaster.

The director of the Edgar Allan Poe House and Museum, along with a few select "grave watchers," patiently man posts inside the warmth of historic Westminster Church. They too want to see the annual ceremonial tribute, but like the outside watchers, no one knows when the expected visitor of the night will arrive.

At some time in the six-hour window, the caller—who is always dressed in black, except for a white scarf that covers his face—secretly enters the churchyard and stops to kneel beside the Poe gravesite. Usually, he pauses to offer a silent prayer, or raise a glass to toast the scribe. On a few occasions, the phantom has left a note with a message behind.

Some observers think the flowers are for each of the three bodies resting beneath the family plot: Edgar; his wife and cousin, Virginia Clemm Poe; and his mother-in-law and aunt, Maria Clemm. No one understands the significance of the French liqueur. Only the mysterious gravesite visitor knows why he created the custom, but he never lingers long enough to engage in conversation.

As decades have passed, speculation has grown that the original "Toaster," who has certainly begun to age or possibly passed on, had been grooming a younger man to continue the touching ritual. Some suggest the original visitor had two sons, and each of them now take turns carrying on the distinctive and colorful Baltimore custom. No matter who the early morning birthday caller is, he returns with regularity on the cold winter morning each January to pay tribute to the master of horror on his birth date, January 19. But, as is appropriate with many of the stories and events related to Poe, the reasons for the ritual and the identities of those involved remain a mystery.

Those unable or unwilling to lurk in the frigid January morning shadows to catch a glimpse of the "Poe Toaster" can visit Poe's gravesite anytime during normal weekday hours. The author's plot,

located in Westminster Cemetery at the busy corner of Greene and Fayette streets in the heart of the city, is easy to find. The distinctive marble monument, with a carved image of Poe, draws the attention of both tourists and passing locals.

On any day there's a good possibility one will find wreaths, individual flowers, bouquets, and even trinkets and coins resting at the base of the tomb. Obviously, some visitors come prepared. Others, seeing the tokens, are inspired to dig into their pockets or purses and join in the custom using whatever they have at hand. Perhaps they want to make their presence known, to feel they've made a connection with the famous writer by leaving something, no matter how slight or trivial, behind.

The preponderance of penny tributes may have some relationship with the grave marker's history. In the late 1800s, Miss Sara Sigourney Rice, a schoolteacher at Baltimore's Western Female High School, organized the effort to provide for a memorial to mark Poe's burial place. To raise funds, she and other teachers encouraged students to contribute "pennies for Poe" and held fundraising events. The monument was dedicated on November 25, 1875, and pennies continue to appear at its base.

In 1849, when his career was somewhat successful, but nothing like it would become after his death, the writer stopped in Baltimore. It is believed he had been traveling on a train from Richmond to New York City. That is when Poe mysteriously disappeared and was found in a delirious state beside a saloon on Lombard Street in the city's Cornbeef Row area. He died four days later in Washington Medical College/Church Home and Hospital, which was closed in 2000. Several theories have been offered as to the how and why of Poe's demise, including rabies, depression, alcoholism, drugs, an enzyme deficiency, a beating by angry potential in-laws, and murder because of unpaid debts or at the hands of Freemasons, to name a few.

Poe was interred in the Old Western Burial Ground (now known as Westminster Cemetery), but his burial plot was located in the rear of the churchyard and was, for the most part, unmarked. His body was moved to the current location at the corner of Greene and Fayette streets in November 1875, twenty-six years after his initial burial. It is said this transfer was executed to accommodate the steady flow of admirers that wanted to visit the original gravesite. A gravestone with the symbol of a raven still marks Poe's first resting place. The newer monument stands in the front of the graveyard.

Not surprisingly, even in death Poe has the ability to generate additional mysteries. Some conspiracy theorists claim grave robbers stole the author's body after his original burial in 1849. Others suggest that Poe is not buried at the second gravesite because the gravediggers pulled up the wrong coffin during the exhumation in 1875. Is it possible that the author still rests below his first tomb that bears a sculpture of a solitary bird, encircled by the famous phrase, "Quoth the Raven Nevermore"? Or are the author's remains long gone, removed by crypt robbers who sold the body soon after the burial? Who will ever know? Like the cause of his death, it's probably another Poe puzzle that will never be solved.

What's Under the Ground?

A large American flag marks Federal Hill and offers a spectacular view of the Inner Harbor and the city of Baltimore to the north. It's believed explorer Captain John Smith ended a short journey at the Patapsco River in 1606 and saw "a great red bank of clay flanking a natural harbor basin." Therefore, early Baltimore settlers called this large mound "John Smith's Hill."

During its history, the well-known landmark has hosted major celebrations, aided maritime commerce and navigation, and served the state and country in times of conflict. During the War of 1812, a signal gun was established at Federal Hill to alert the city and harbor about potential British attack, but since the British advances failed at both Fort McHenry and Hampstead Hill (now a city park called Patterson Park), the Federal Hill artillery guns were not fired. Immediately after the Baltimore Riots in April 1861—when Baltimore's Southern sympathizers attacked Union troops near the President Street Railroad Station—Federal forces occupied the hill and established barricades and artillery at what became known as Federal Hill Fort.

The site was turned into a public city park in 1880, and in the 1970s the surrounding neighborhood, identified as "Federal Hill District," was named to the National Register of Historic Places.

Today the Federal Hill area remains popular, accented by restored homes, as well as restaurants, taverns, and shops that are patronized by tourists and residents.

But Federal Hill also has its own legend, an urban legend spread by friend-of-a-friend (FOAF) gossip and embellished over the years. And since an element of truth is usually the basis for any good story, the facts about the Federal Hill tunnels lie, literally, beneath the surface of the "great red bank of clay."

During the nineteenth century, miners dug short tunnels under and into the large hill to extract fine white sand used to make glass. Workers also hauled away red clay and used it for sash weights for windows, and some can still be found in the nearby neighborhood structures.

Through the Civil War, the Union troops stored gunpowder in the tunnels beneath Fort Federal Hill. But tales were told that there are remnants of these Civil War passageways—which extended from Federal Hill to nearby Fort McHenry. There also are reports that the tunnels extended all the way to Fort Carroll (located in the middle of the Patapsco River) and to the Washington Monument (across the Inner Harbor, in the center of the city).

In the book *Baltimore Ghosts: History, Mystery, Legends and Lore*, Vince Vaise, a park ranger at Fort McHenry, made this comment: "They said the Union troops used the subterranean passages to secretly go from one place to another. But, since the Union troops controlled the city, they didn't have to use tunnels. If anything, it would have been the Confederates who needed to travel secretly and make use of such a large and mysterious underground network."

Vince said that the legends of the tunnels gained some credibility in the 1950s, when a row house near Federal Hill caved into one of the old mining tunnels. Despite denials and explanations that it would be physically impossible for the tunnels to be long enough to reach all of the mentioned sites—and that they would have to be dug under the shipping channels—some people still believe they exist on a grand scale.

Many of the reports have been spread as Baltimore's very own urban legend for generations. Oftentimes, when believers in the extensive tunnel passageways are corrected, they accuse historians of being part of a government conspiracy to cover up the tunnels' existence.

According to the website Federal Hill Online, because the tunnels are cool, nearby breweries stored kegs of beer at the site. But rumors persist of children having been lost in the underground labyrinths and of the hidden passageways that were used during Prohibition to hide and transport illegal booze.

Even today, those with creative imaginations claim that in the basements of homes and in the cellars of old businesses—behind boarded up entranceways—there are secret mazes that will lead you to Fort McHenry, Baltimore's Washington Monument, and who knows where else within and beyond Charm City.

Secretive Spirits at Fells Point

It's often said Fells Point comes alive at night, as clubs and saloons offer entertainment and dining specials. On any weekend, moving throngs of couples and groups crowd the historic sidewalks, heading from pub to inn. A buzz of excitement fills the air, and it doesn't end until early in the darkness of the morning. And that's when some believe the ghosts come out.

But before we deal with tales of phantoms and mystery, let's put this hot-spot, place-to-be-seen urban center into perspective. In the early 1700s, the hub of Baltimore was located east of today's Inner Harbor tourist zone. Numerous bars, boarding houses, brothels, and boatyards formed a waterfront community established by the Fells, a family of merchants and shipbuilders. The shipping business and up to eighteen shipbuilding yards attracted an odd assortment of characters—ranging from wealthy landowners and businessmen to deck hands and artisans, plus those who made their living serving food and drink and offering entertainment. To those returning from or heading out to sea, the village named after William Fell was the place to be.

An English immigrant, Fell founded the site between 1726 and 1730, recognizing its value as a deepwater port. In the 1770s, William's son, Edward Fell, laid out the streets and gave them English names such as Thames and Shakespeare, many of which exist to this day.

Fells Point shipbuilding increased dramatically during the American Revolution, and the industry would continue for a number of decades. During the War of 1812, more American ships were needed, and the Fells Point shipyards were kept busy with orders from Congress. When shipbuilding declined in the 1830s, the area became known as a warehousing center. Later, maritime steam engines overshadowed sail power, and the wooden shipbuilders at Fells Point were sucked into a long downward spiral that would change their lives and livelihood. By 1960, more than 225 years since its optimistic beginnings, the area was showing signs of urban neglect. But two decades of community effort and the establishment of preservation societies enabled the neighborhood to survive, restore many of its buildings, and turn Fells Point into a desirable residential neighborhood—as well as a living history center and tourist attraction.

But some believe that along the cobblestone streets, and within the walls of old bars and boarding houses, those who played a role in the neighborhood's colorful history have remained. Some residents and business owners believe that, at times, these souls from the past actually can make their presence known. If that is correct, there are probably ghost stories on every corner and in every old structure and saloon within Fells Point. Here are just a few.

In Bertha's bar and restaurant, constructed sometime between 1770 and 1820, paranormal activity has been noted in the upstairs apartment, where a tenant's cat would freeze its motion to a halt, and the animal's fur would stand up across its back. It would remain that way and not move a muscle for an unusually long period of time.

Another area on that floor hosts a spacious dance studio, with a large mirror-covered wall. An employee walking through the dance studio at 6 A.M. saw a figure of a woman in the mirror, dressed in black with a big hat. The worker thought "it was an actual visage of a person." There also has been a sighting of a male figure in a large hat and dark cloak standing on the nearby stairway.

A member of the wait staff reported a sighting involving a little girl, standing or skipping and causing a rhythmic sound in a corner on the second floor. When a local paranormal group conducted an investigation, a member noted the spirit of a little girl, upstairs in a storeroom near a window. It's believed that the area of the sighting was once a closet, during the period when the building was a brothel. Possibly, the spirit of the girl still stands where she had been told to hide and remain by her mother, who may have been dealing with an irate customer.

An out-of-town family having lunch asked if the place was "haunted." After the waiter replied, "This whole neighborhood is haunted. This is the most haunted part of town," the startled man pointed to a spot nearby, identified as Table #5. The tourist said he saw an older man, dressed in overalls and with a beard, smoking a pipe. The man looked like a fisherman. But, when a customer walked past, the old fisherman just disappeared.

Visitors to the Cat's Eye Pub take note of its "Wall of Death," featuring photos of former employees and customers that have passed on. Bar regulars admit to occasions when the place "gets a bit spirited." In particular, there's a history of things—model ships and pictures—falling off the walls and some flying across the room. Sometimes it seems they are targeting certain individuals. One occasion involved a bartender who had been talking unflatteringly about a former owner. Within a few moments, a small photograph dropped off the wall and landed on her head.

The Whistling Oyster, a saloon featured in the History Channel documentary *Haunted Baltimore,* claims a fair amount of unexplained activity. "There are spirits in this bar that are not contained in bottles," owner Read Hopkins said in a 2004 interview.

The oldest part of the building dates to the 1760s. Some of the early owners had slaves, but they lived about a block away. Perhaps one of the slaves found his way back and appeared in modern times, since a customer reported seeing a black man in Colonial-era attire sweeping the floor near the fireplace.

A small storage closet stands against the wall between the front bar and the back room. Previously, a set of stairs leading to the second floor stood in this area. People have heard phantom footsteps from the site where the original stairs have been removed.

One night an ash bucket appeared in the aisle near the fireplace. Each time it was moved off to the side, the bucket reappeared in the pathway, blocking the flow of foot traffic. Eventually, the bucket returned there so many times that no one wanted to touch it and put it in its proper place.

In the book *Baltimore Ghosts: History, Mystery, Legends and Lore,* Read offered a possible explanation for the unusual events that have occurred at the Whistling Oyster. His words, however, might aptly apply to the many other spirited inns located throughout Fells Point.

"I know a lot of people come here who haven't been in town for a long time, and they had a good time so they come back here." Read continued, "It could be that people die and want to come back to a place where they had a good time, and that's right here."

Along Shakespeare Street, people have reported seeing the figure of a man, wearing dated clothing. Some think it may be someone from a period long ago. This finely dressed but rather filmy apparition makes his way along the narrow lane, heading west, away from Broadway and then he . . . disappears. Some believe it is the ghost of one of the founders of Fells Point. To many the explanation seems to have some merit.

A small plot, surrounded by a wrought iron fence, is the final resting place of four members of the Fell family—Edward and William; and Williams's son Edward and grandson William. The granite marker was placed here in 1927 to mark the founders' family plot. Some believe a mansion stood nearby, but that is long gone, as are the shipyards, the slaves, the clipper ships, and the wooden-hulled warships.

But the spirits of the Fells—and the sailors and sweethearts, immigrants and craftsmen, harlots and merchants—and all who worked at Fells Point before it became the tourist destination it is today, well, maybe a few of them have remained. And, like the spirits of the Fells, they too may take quiet walks along the streets on lonely nights, recalling days long gone by.

Medical Grave Robbers

There's a state historical marker at the busy intersection of Greene and Lombard streets. The metal sign stands beside the steps leading to Davidge Hall, the columned and domed nineteenth-century building named for Dr. John B. Davidge, first dean of Maryland's first medical school. The old-fashioned marker refers to the hall being the "oldest building in the country used continuously for medical education . . ." and states that the medical school, "established in 1807 by the Maryland General Assembly, was the fifth to be founded in the United States. . . ."

While interesting and informative, based on these details Davidge Hall is not a site that the average seeker of legends, lore, or ghost stories would place on even a Top-1,000 list. But looks—and historical markers, in particular—can be deceiving and very, very boring.

For the purposes of our book, Davidge Hall, which now serves as home of the Medical Alumni Association of the University of Maryland, was one of the East Coast centers for grave robbing. (Now, isn't that more interesting than the dates and data on the plaque?)

This chapter focuses on the practices and controversy that centered on the dead bodies that nineteenth-century physicians needed for dissections and research. But as Larry Pitrof, executive director of the medical college's alumni association, explained in the book *Baltimore Ghosts: History, Mystery, Legends and Lore,* when the medical school began in the early 1800s, doctors had not attained the level of respect and prestige they hold today. At that time, medicine was unregulated and those who were ill sought relief from barbershop surgeons, street corner apothecaries, men of the cloth who were believed to possess healing abilities, and neighborhood practitioners of folk medicine.

Also, most people believed that when a person died, the body needed to be buried where it would rest undisturbed until the Resurrection. If anyone dared slice open a corpse for medical examination, its soul would escape and the recently deceased would be doomed to wander restlessly forever.

To fill a need for bodies for medical study, staff and officials at the nineteenth-century University of Maryland were involved in body snatching, but they were not alone. The practice occurred at other medical schools throughout America and in Europe. In fact, grave robbing was so rampant in Ireland that snipers were placed in watchtowers surrounding cemeteries. Their job was to shoot bands of grave robbers that would make money from digging up and selling a fresh corpse.

Baltimore physicians practiced their craft and performed secret autopsies in their homes; however, when the neighbors found out, the results were unpleasant. Riots occurred and mobs gathered to express their disapproval. Eventually, the historic medical school at Greene and Lombard streets was built in what was a rural area so that the medical community's activities at that time could be conducted a distance from the center of town—and, therefore, less subject to the scrutiny of angry city residents.

It wasn't until the 1880s that Maryland law permitted agencies to turn over unclaimed bodies, and those of deceased criminals, to the college for medical research. In the interim, teaching doctors and researchers had to resort to other means of finding cadavers to educate students in anatomy. But the fact remains that from approximately 1807 to the 1880s, grave robbing proved to be an illegal, but necessary and workable, option. It was also convenient because, within walking distance of the medical college, a number of nearby cemeteries offered a steady supply of cadavers to meet the educational demand.

"We were robbing graves at Westminster Burying Ground and anywhere else we could get cadavers," Pitrof said. He added that in recent years, "Frank the Grave Robber" has been the name used to represent a composite image of all of the body snatchers employed and used by the Maryland medical college, which, at that time, was paying about $20 for a body. "It's believed students also participated in the practice," he added, "and there even were professional grave robbers who were available for hire."

No doubt a variety of methods were used to discover a fresh corpse and then extricate the body efficiently from its "eternal" resting place. Frank would follow the horse-drawn hearse and funeral procession to the graveyard and observe the scene, paying close attention to the position of the body as it was lowered into the ground. (This was critical to the speedy and efficient late-evening removal of the corpse.)

Under cover of darkness, the grave robber would arrive at the plot and carefully note the position of any special items of tribute that had been placed atop the mound by family and friends. These would be replaced in the proper order after the body was removed to cover up evidence of the nighttime robber's visit. Since he had noted the position of the corpse as it was placed at the cemetery ceremony, the snatcher dug up only the portion of the grave above the head of the coffin. When his spade reached the box, he smashed open the lid and used a curved, butcher-style meat hook—which was placed under the cadaver's chin—to yank the prize swiftly from the hole in the earth. Within minutes, the body was out of the ground. After replacing the dirt and returning the mementos to their proper position, Frank would toss the body over a shoulder and race with it through back alleys and along dimly lit streets, arriving at the side doors of Davidge Hall.

According to the History Channel documentary *Secret Passages,* when renovations were conducted at nearby Westminster Church, workmen who had to dig foundations for the church in the old graveyard reported that several of the graves in the Burying Ground were empty. While Westminster Church was convenient, being only two blocks from the medical school, body snatchers also raided other city cemeteries.

To be useful for anatomical dissections, Pitrof explained, the bodies had to be "fresh" and, therefore, secured soon after burial. Knowing this, cemeteries built walls to keep grave robbers out. Also, families hired guards that would stand beside new gravesites, remaining on watch until enough time had passed for decomposition to begin. This was done to protect loved ones from being carted off. (Embalming did not come into practice until the Civil War.)

Frank, the grave robber, and his colleagues carried their cadaver contraband up a narrow, winding stairway to the third floor of Davidge Hall. Today, in a cramped alcove hidden from the main hallway on the building's top floor, an old wooden barrel stands beside the edge of the staircase. Pitrof explained that the wooden container is a replica of the all-purpose barrels that were used to store and also ship dead bodies. Dissections were conducted in this confined area near the barrel, and the appropriate organs were removed for study, which would take place in the nearby amphitheater, named Anatomical Hall.

The Maryland college's janitorial staff by day—and grave-robbing operators by night—was very proficient. They were so good at their part-time job that local bodies were sold and shipped to schools in need of cadavers as far away as New England. A letter dated September 25, 1830—from Dr. Nathan R. Smith, professor of surgery at Maryland, to Dr. Parker Cleaveland of Bowdoin College in Maine—praises the proficiency of the Baltimore grave-robbing staff. Dr. Smith promises delivery of several "subjects" that will be shipped north in "barrels of whiskey." The Maryland doctor stated he would enlist the assistance of "Frank, our body-snatcher (a better man never lifted a spade), and confer with him on the matter."

Since police and family scrutiny of the medical school staff was highest immediately after a funeral, Larry Pitrof said that sometimes Frank would have to hide the body for a short time. To preserve the specimen until it was safe to make delivery, the corpse would be stuffed into a barrel filled with whiskey. After the body was removed from the alcohol-filled keg, Frank would sell the whiskey to unknowing local saloonkeepers or to naïve medical students—hence the origin of the term "rot gut whiskey."

According to Larry, even though the grave robbing continued with some regularity for nearly eighty years, there were no prosecutions. In light of the public's and law enforcement's awareness of the practice, that seems hard to believe. "It was incredible," Pitrof said. "It would have made today's drug smugglers look like children."

Many might expect college officials to try to cover up the gruesome past associated with Davidge Hall, but instead, present administrators speak openly about the school's history. Several representatives' candid comments are featured in the History Channel documentary. Addressing this issue, Pitrof said, "We're obligated to tell the true story of medicine here. It may not always be rosy and fuzzy. But it's a part of our lives and we shouldn't ignore it. Today, the medical profession is associated with prestige, acceptance, and validation. When students enter into medical education, they are introduced to cadavers and know they are plentiful, and it's noble to dissect a body for medical science. Many don't realize that two hundred years ago there was a black-market operation to secure what they take for granted today."

Annapolis and the Chesapeake Bay

MARYLAND'S COLONIAL CAPITAL CITY OFFERS SPIRITED SIGHTINGS extending to the earliest days of our country. But the nearby Chesapeake Bay has an even longer legacy, one associated with pirates, treasure, superstitions, and its very own sea monster—Chessie—who puts in an appearance from time to time.

Last Dance

Bad luck and tragedy seem to have been associated with the site of Maryland's State House. The first building, erected in 1697, lasted only two years when lightning struck and the resulting fire damaged the structure. Fire returned in the early 1700s and caused more destruction. A second State House was finished in 1709, but it lasted about sixty years before more room was needed and planning began for a larger replacement.

Work on the third—and present—capitol started in 1772, but the war for independence delayed its completion until 1779. Today, Maryland's State House claims to be the oldest U.S. state capitol building still in continuous legislative use. It also has a more prestigious distinction, being the first peacetime capitol of the United States, and it is the only state capitol building that also served as the nation's capitol. George Washington, in his role of America's general, visited the building to resign his commission as commander in chief of America's Revolutionary army.

Modern tourists visiting historic Annapolis are drawn to the State Circle, where the State House stands. Certainly, a large part of this attention is due to the attractive building's impressive wooden tiered dome and acorn-shaped top projecting toward the sky. Once inside the building, those on guided tours are impressed by these architectural achievements and find their eyes instinctively drawn toward the top of the building's dome.

But some in the tour group have no interest in the handcrafted moldings, wooden pegs, and artistic ironwork. They're hoping to get a glimpse or capture a picture of the building's resident ghost—Thomas Dance. According to legend, in 1793, Dance was busy at work, plastering the top of the dome, when he fell nearly one hundred feet, crashing against the ground below. Over the years, there have been reports of a mysterious figure roaming the capitol grounds, areas within the building, and, of course, at sites near the interior and exterior of the building dome, where Dance had been working when he died suddenly. As expected, as years passed, any sudden noise, gusty breeze, sudden chill, mysterious shadow, or unexplained event has been attributed to the unfortunate plasterer—who never finished his task on the state capitol dome because he took an unplanned "last dance."

Ghostly Procession

While many old cities have haunted houses, Annapolis is able to boast of its "haunted street." The legend is connected to Sir Robert Eden, the last English governor that served under King George and who administered the colony from 1769 to 1776. In June, just before the signing of the Declaration of Independence, Governor Eden hurriedly abandoned his goods and property and sailed back to England aboard a British warship docked off Annapolis harbor. After the end of the Revolutionary War, in 1784, the former royal governor returned to the Maryland capital, and he was greeted with a mixed reception, since in his official days he had been friendly with both American rebels and English loyalists. It's said Eden's final days in the former colony were uneventful, since he was astute enough to keep a low profile, for anti-British sentiment was still high in the decades following the conflict.

Upon his death, friends decided that the corpse might be the target of vengeful patriots. To prevent desecration or theft of the governor's body, they decided it would be best if the official was buried with little fanfare and in a less prominent location than St. Anne's Cemetery, which is located in the middle of the Maryland capital. Under darkness, Eden's coffin was carried down Shipwright Street to a waiting craft at Spa Creek. Once aboard, it was transported outside of town to St. Margaret's Churchyard for interment. But nearly 150 years later, Eden's coffin and remains were exhumed and brought back into Annapolis. Today, the last British governor rests in peace in St. Anne's Cemetery.

Some say that a ghostly procession—recreating the funeral walk that silently secreted Eden's spirited soul out of town—is repeated on dark, fog-shrouded nights. Witnesses report that the slaves carrying their master's coffin and others guiding the way with glowing lanterns make no sound, as their bare feet slap silently along historic Shipwright Street heading toward the water—into which the procession disappears.

John Paul Jones, Home at Last

There was a special ceremony held at the U.S. Naval Academy in Annapolis on July 9, 2005, marking the one-hundredth anniversary of the return of the body of John Paul Jones from France on July 22, 1905. But the route the American Revolutionary War naval hero took to arrive at a final resting place in his adopted country is one that spans several continents, an ocean, and more than one hundred years.

Jones is well known for uttering the most famous phrase in U.S. naval history: "I have not yet begun to fight." It occurred when a British captain demanded that the American sailor surrender his sinking ship and cease fire. Ignoring the command and continuing the battle, Jones's ship, the *Bonhomme Richard*, was sunk, but Jones and his crew were victorious and took over the British ship HMS *Serapis* in a battle off the coast of England on September 23, 1779.

Born in Scotland on July 6, 1747, Jones came to the American colonies at the age of twenty-six and received a commission in the Continental Navy, where he subsequently commanded four ships. He never lost a battle and was known for his courage and warrior-like spirit. However, when the colonies defeated Great Britain, Jones longed for more action. So he followed the watery battlefields, serving in the navies of both Russia and France. On July 18, 1792, in failing health and relatively poor, he died in Paris.

In his book *After the Funeral: The Posthumous Adventures of Famous Corpses,* Edwin Murphy details the long series of mishaps that occurred to the corpse of America's famed naval hero. Since Jones was rather unpopular and without liquid assets or easily accessible wealth, his death was ignored by the U.S. minister to France, and the American sailor was buried in a Protestant cemetery about four miles outside of Paris. However, upon hearing of the indignity, the French government stepped in and gave Jones a hero's reburial and preserved his corpse in alcohol in a lead coffin lined with straw.

Meanwhile, in the United States, there seemed to be no interest in the fate of the deceased hero, although a ship was named after Jones in 1834. In the late 1800s, a journalist began making inquiries and learned that the site of the cemetery outside Paris was now part of Paris, and the general area of the lost graveyard was covered with buildings. According to www.seacoastnh.com, "The cemetery had been covered over by a grocery store, a laundry, an apartment house, sheds, cess pools, and wells."

Eventually, when the housing site was later condemned, an excavation was conducted to locate the lost admiral, with workers spending weeks tunneling through old basements, caverns, and beneath the city's ancient streets. Much of the effort to locate and identify Jones's remains was led by General Horace Porter, who was appointed American ambassador to France in 1899. When five lead coffins were discovered, the records that indicated Jones had been preserved in alcohol and tucked in with straw helped the searchers locate the correct lost corpse. The body was discovered on April 8, 1905. Later, an autopsy, along with a comparison of the remains to details of a bust created years earlier by sculptor Jean-Antoine Houdon, confirmed the corpse to be that of the American naval officer.

With an American flag draped across a wooden coffin, Jones was honored with a parade through Paris. At the port of Cherbourg, nearly a dozen naval craft of both France and the United States escorted the "Father of the American Navy" to his final resting place—a grand sepulcher at the U.S. Naval Academy chapel in Annapolis. His body arrived in Maryland on July 22, 1905. And there he waited, to be buried yet again.

Since Congress had not appropriated the funds, there was no tomb, and the corpse sat in a storage room in the basement of Bancroft Hall for a year until the official, grand "welcome home" ceremony was held on April 24, 1906. On that day, before a crowd of more than a thousand, there were speeches by the governor of Maryland, who welcomed Jones home to rest in the Free State; by the U.S. ambassador to France, who talked of the discovery and recovery of the hero's long-lost body; and by U.S. President Theodore Roosevelt, who spoke of the importance of a strong naval fleet. And the audience cheered.

Then Jones was hauled back into the basement of Bancroft Hall, for Congress still had not acted to approve funding for his crypt. It would be six years later, on January 26, 1913, when John Paul Jones had his final (fourth or fifth, but who's counting?) burial, in an ornate, marble sarcophagus, located in the lower level of the Naval Academy chapel.

One would think that the story ends here, and for most people it does. But there are still those who question if the body in the magnificent mausoleum is really that of John Paul Jones. Some historians periodically suggest that the crypt be opened and that a DNA sample from the hero's remains be compared with that of his siblings, whose burial sites are known—just to be sure. Naval Academy spokespersons have been quoted as stating that there is no question regarding the identity of the corpse and that there are no plans to disturb the remains. Most folks would tend to agree. After all, shouldn't we let his restless soul rest in peace, at last?

Navy Bombs Island Ghost

It was before World War II in 1938, when the U.S. Navy aimed its resources on a deserted Chesapeake Bay island to prepare its future officers for impending naval combat. The strange scenario was reported on May 10 in the *Baltimore Sun,* under the headlines: "U.S. Navy Prepares To Bomb Lone Ghost of Sharps Island" and "Spook Warned To Seek Shelter, as Midshipmen Will Use Place for Practice."

Sharps Island at the mouth of the Eastern Shore's Choptank River had been deserted for years. In order to provide second-year midshipmen from the U.S. Naval Academy at Annapolis with bombing practice, the island was rented from its owners so that a squadron of twin-motored patrol ships could conduct firing exercises with trainees—using bombs filled with water rather than explosives.

Apparently, the excitement over the impending invasion rekindled tales of the ghost that was believed to roam the deserted island, which had once been populated by summer vacationers who stayed in a spacious hotel and numerous summer cottages. Through the late 1890s, Sharps Island was a getaway destination and also a popular site for duck hunters, but only a few folks lived there year-round.

Erosion and a rising sea level were the cause of the island's demise, and as the residents departed, they left formerly useful buildings behind. Left unattended, the structures slowly were claimed by the rising Chesapeake waters and spreading island vegetation; however, before Mother Nature finished her work, scavengers returned to Sharps to cart off anything of value, and useful remnants of the island's buildings began appearing in homes and structures on the mainland. About this time is when reports of the island ghost began to spread. The stories were based on sightings of nighttime shadows and folks declaring they were hearing bumps in the deserted buildings at night. Eventually, only the stone foundations and the ghost stories remained.

But there was one other myth associated with Sharps Island, based on a story told during the Civil War era in the nearby town of Cambridge. It seems the originator of the tale said he dreamed there was buried treasure on Sharps, and he claimed to know of its exact location. Initially, he was the subject of laughter, but a few days later the scoffers changed their tune. The old fellow, it's said, bought the entire island using several gold coins that were enough to seal the deal—and he never shared the source of his sudden wealth.

The island is now deserted, the town and the old screwpile-style light building are long gone, the latter destroyed by ice floes in 1881. The red metal lighthouse in the Bay stands as a reminder of a one thousand-acre island that has since been reduced to less than a hundred acres. But that's still more than enough room on which a solitary ghost may roam.

Floating Coffin of Hooper Island

There's a Chesapeake Bay tale associated with Hooper Island, located at the western edge of Dorchester County, where the land ends and the water rules. It was probably in old general stores and rural post offices or perhaps on decks of rocking ships or near fishing holes that yarns and tales were shared as residents anticipated arrival of mail, waited out sudden storms, or watched for nibbles on a fishing line.

Life near the marshland and along the guts and islands required perseverance and ingenuity, particularly for those working on the open water and living alongside the soggy land. Things that city and country folk took for granted demanded different attention by the water folk, such as burying their dead. With the high water table exerting significant pressure, coffins of the deceased were buried in high ground; however, in island graveyards, which are never far from surrounding water, the boxes of the dead are placed to rest in graves above the surface. While decorative boxlike monuments enclose these bodies, there is no guarantee that the dearly departed will remain there forever. Such is the tale of the Floating Coffin.

According to a *Baltimore Sun* article published on Halloween Day, 1972—and written by reporters Joseph J. Challmes and Tom Horton—this eerie event occurred during the Great Storm of 1933. Others suggest it happened many years earlier, and some even claim the creepy circumstances took place along the southern Atlantic Coast or somewhere in New England. But while variations of this water village folktale may differ slightly in certain locales, the gist remains the same.

A sudden fierce storm delivered wave upon rising wave of water onto the saturated island. An aging waterman was trapped on the upper floor of his cabin, waiting for the most certain arrival of his last earthly visitor—a rain-soaked Shadow of Death. With no hope of escape, the old salt had made his peace with the Lord, and the fisherman resigned his inevitable fate to the hands of King Neptune and Davy Jones.

Amidst the howling wind and splattering rain, which sounded like gunshots hitting his roof, the waterman heard a steady tapping against the second-floor window. Over and over the slow rhythmic beating occurred, as if in sync with the crashing waves and surging gusts of the deadly storm. Eventually, the captive sailor crawled to the window, its base now level with the height of the threatening water. Having trouble seeing through the darkness of the night, he pulled up the window, and a wooden coffin floated into the second-floor room. He immediately recognized the long narrow box, for it contained the corpse of his recently deceased wife, who had been interred in the island graveyard. Some say the waterman opened the lid and the dead wife, stiffened with rigor mortis, sat half upright. Others claim the old man dared not raise the top of the coffin and was satisfied to read his wife's name that had been burned into the top panel.

In either case, the old salt shoved the well-built walnut box out the second-floor window, climbed aboard, and both rode *and* rowed his makeshift, life-saving craft throughout the stormy night, arriving safely on an adjacent island. There's no logical explanation for the series of events that allowed the doomed man to survive being swept to sea. And locals used to swear that the tale that extended his life for several years beyond the Great Storm was absolutely true. Some even added with a sly smirk that upon arriving on dry land, the relieved waterman proclaimed: "Thanks, old woman! You always did look after me."

Chessie

Nessie, the sea monster from Loch (Lake) Ness in Scotland, is known around the world as the most famous sea serpent, with scores of reports of the creature noted as early as the sixth century.

Sightings in the 1930s rejuvenated interest, and over the years blurred photographs and scientific expeditions, along with cable television feature segments, have placed Loch Ness on the tourist map. Each year, thousands head to the Scottish lake to try to get a glimpse of the elusive sea monster. Believers suggest that the depth of Loch Ness, and its large size (twenty-two square miles), may offer conditions that can sustain the appetite and habitat of a large, mysterious underwater creature.

But Nessie is not alone. Sea monsters have been sighted for thousands of years, and in the New World since the 1600s. In recent years, there have been reports from sea captains, sailors, and water-village residents, as well as recreational and commercial fishermen. Depending upon its geographical location and the body of water it calls home, these creatures go by various names: Champ in Lake Champlain; Ogopogo in Lake Okanagan, British Columbia; South Bay Bessie in Lake Erie; White River Monster in Newport, Arkansas; Slimy Slim in Lake Payette, Idaho; Tessie in Lake Tahoe, California; and Chessie in the Chesapeake Bay, to list only a few.

These snakelike creatures that pop their heads above the water's surface have been estimated to have lengths of a mere dozen feet to up to two hundred feet. They are elusive, easily mistaken for other water inhabitants or even shadows and driftwood. Still—in spite of the lack of scientific proof and the threat of public humiliation for those who share their experiences—reports continue to surface periodically.

According to the Maryland Department of Natural Resources (MDNR) website, one of the earliest reports of Chessie was made "in 1936 when a military helicopter flew over the Bush River. The crew reported seeing something reptilian and unknown in the water. Reports of Chessie were not common until the 1980s."

The front page of the *Baltimore Evening Sun*'s September 17, 1980, issue featured a sketch of the serpent by Trudy Guthrie. The headline "'Creature' Is Said To Rise from Bay" grabbed readers' attention. In the accompanying story from Stevensville, Trudy and her husband, Coleman Guthrie, said they saw a "creature" in the waters between Tilghman and Bennett points. "While the creature remained unidentified," Bill Burton, *Evening Sun* outdoor editor, wrote, "she said it was big, definitely alive, and unlike anything she and her husband ever saw." The story continued with Trudy, a former boating columnist, stating, "We both saw six to eight feet of it from the head back, but there obviously was more of it. We saw no end to it, though we got a good close-up look for four or five seconds."

A later story by Burton in the October 21, 1980, issue was head-lined "Watermen Report More Sightings of Bay Creature." According to MDNR, in May of 1982, the first hard evidence of Chessie's existence arrived from videotape made by the Frew family, who spotted the serpentlike creature near their Kent Island (northern Chesapeake Bay) home. Later that summer, the MDNR reported, "the Smithsonian had a minisymposium to determine if the video-tape was indeed evidence of Chessie's existence." Someone also produced a picture at the sessions. The owner said she had previously been hesitant to share it in public.

According to Jerome Clark, in his book *Unexplained: 347 Strange Sightings, Incredible Occurrences, and Puzzling Physical Phenomena,* the Chesapeake Bay creature sighted in 1982 by Robert and Karen Frew was described as snakelike and was estimated to be about thirty-five feet long. Clark noted that the Smithsonian's National Museum of Natural History, in a subsequent report on the scientific group's analysis of Frew's videotape, acknowledged that the object seemed to be alive, could not be identified, and added that similar sightings "have been reported regularly for a the past several years."

In the summer of 1984, there were a slew of Chessie sightings—on August 4, 9, and 14—which took place in the middle and southern reaches of the Bay. These prompted attention-grabbing headlines in the *Kent Island Bay Times:* "Chessie Sighted: Third Consecutive Week," "Chessie Seen Again Near Eastern Bay," "Chessie Gives Encore Appearance: Now Seen by Watermen," and "Jumpin Catfish . . . It's Chessie Again!" In the last story, Lisa Lister, the paper's managing editor, wrote: "There is something 'humongous' out there swimming in the waters of the Eastern Bay off Kent Island. Could it be 'Chessie?'"

Some newspaper reports suggested that the "creature" had been confused with the remnants of a dead manatee, measuring about nine feet, which apparently had starved to death, since the Bay does not offer the proper vegetation it needs to survive. But several other Chessie reports, followed up that hectic summer by editor Lister, stated the creature had a serpentlike appearance. One witness described it as "large, bluish-black and had three humps out of the water."

"Elusive 'Chessie' Stumps Computer" was a summer 1984 *Baltimore Sun* headline, referring to results of an examination of the original 1982 Frew family videotape by Johns Hopkins University's Applied Physics Laboratory. Referred to as the "Chesapeake Bay Phenomenon," some of the researchers involved were convinced "there is a live, unidentified creature prowling the waters of the Chesapeake Bay." This finding is similar to the research conducted two years earlier. While no physical evidence had been found—and with sailors, boaters, residents, scientists, and tourists all reading the sensational, front-page headlines and details—it's not surprising that Chessie mania was rampant during the mid-1980s.

In recent years, reports of Chessie sightings have subsided, but that has not stopped the stories from continuing. Like most regional legends, Maryland's "Chessie" name has been commercialized and can be found in tourist area gift shops printed on mugs, T-shirts, and key chains. Of course, increased use of the serpent's clever, Chesapeake Bay–connected name helps perpetuate belief in the serpent's existence.

To those skeptics that believe the Chesapeake sea serpent reports are nothing more than the imagination of tired fishermen or the hopes of delusional believers, it's worth keeping a few facts in mind. Periodically, all-knowing, practical scientists—who often state they have identified every living creature on the planet—admit their astonishment when a new species of bird, insect, or fish is discovered. Loch Ness, reported home of Nessie, is a mere twenty-two square miles and up to 740 feet deep. The Chesapeake Bay, Chessie's habitat, is quite a bit larger, more than four thousand square miles and up to 175 feet deep. Certainly, with that much area and with a southern access point leading directly into the Atlantic Ocean, the existence of Maryland's sea serpent might be more than just a hopeful dream; it might be a distinct possibility.

Sea Superstitions Can't Hurt

Chesapeake Bay fishermen, vacationers, and residents are aware of the abundance of legends associated with sea serpents, ghost ships, floating specters, and unexplained bay sightings that have been passed down for generations. More important, perhaps, is the role of folklore in superstitions, which are followed by those who work the waters and which often focus on how to protect oneself from deadly spirits of the deep. Following are a number of sea superstitions that have survived, in some instances, for hundreds of years.

Tossing a coin overboard before heading out from the dock is giving Neptune, god of the sea, his tribute and helps ensure a safe voyage. Also, placing coins under the mast will bring good luck and favorable winds. Pouring a shot of whiskey, particularly rum, overboard—or pouring wine on the deck—will help satisfy the needs of the water spirits and secure good luck. (While this is to be done on a maiden voyage, some resort to using liquid spirits each time they leave port.)

Tossing salt into the sea will ensure a good fishing catch, and throwing the first fish caught back into the sea will bring good luck and produce future large catches. Years ago, the first fish caught was nailed to the mast. On a boat's first voyage, it is good luck to throw a shoe into the ship's wake. This is similar to shoes and cans tied behind the bridal car at a wedding, but shoes, when taken off, must not land upside down on deck. This is bad luck, since a shoe resembles a boat, and a turned-up shoe predicts the boat also will capsize.

If a crow flies across a boat, it's a sign of bad luck; but if two or more happen to fly across a craft, it predicts a good day's catch. The screeches of birds are bad luck, representing the cries of former shipmates returned from the dead. Bringing a live bird on a boat is bad luck, but if a bird lands on a boat while at sea, it is good luck. However, a black bird landing on a boat approaching shore is a sign that bad luck is near.

Cats on a boat make old mariners edgy, for they believe the animals are an alternative life-form of a witch and will bring bad luck. In some cases, cats were taken to sea, but their activities were watched very carefully. If the animal became agitated, disappeared, or fell overboard, it was a sign that a storm was approaching and that the ship was doomed.

When the sea winds died and the air was still, sailing ship mariners believed they could generate a breeze to fill the sails by whistling. However, they were careful not to offer too spirited a tune, for they did not want a dangerous gale but only a steady wind to help the wooden sailing ship along. Some captains hired a witch or magician to come on the voyage, and if the sea winds failed for too long a period, the hired mystic would conjure up a breeze to move the vessel along its course.

Blue is a bad-luck color for a boat because that color belongs to the water gods. Indians believed that if they used blue, it would make the water gods jealous and unhappy, and some fishermen head back to shore if they discover anything bearing the color blue on their boat. Watermen are careful to avoid the use of walnut in the construction of boats. Traditionally, this dark wood was used for coffins; if used to repair a boat, the craft will experience bad luck.

The Irish say a banshee cannot cross water. On the Chesapeake Bay, some believe this legend applies to ghosts and spirits that are trapped on the many islands scattered in and around the Bay. Sailors murdered at sea will not rest until their killer has been found and punished.

Slaves and their immediate descendants were particularly fearful of dolphins, since they thought the creatures would call out the names of those traveling on nearby ships. To satisfy the cries of these sea creatures, those persons named would be tossed overboard as a sacrifice to the sea.

Never leave port on a Friday; this is the day Christ was crucified and died. Also, don't sail from port on the thirteenth day of the month. Since they dress in black, priests are unlucky travelers on a ship, and black traveling bags are unlucky for a sailor.

Women on board are back luck, since their presence makes the sea angry. They also distract sailors from their duties and cause fatal accidents and shipwrecks. However, a naked woman on board calms the sea. This is why naked figureheads are carved on the bow of ships. Having contact with red-haired people or flat-footed people is bad luck; avoid them before you sail. If a child is born on board, it brings that boat good luck and is considered a blessing and ensures a safe voyage.

A ship should be boarded right foot first, and from the right (starboard) side. The words drowned, egg, rabbit, pig, salt, and the number 13 will bring bad luck if spoken on a ship at sea. Tossing a stone over a craft will curse it and doom its return from the voyage, and it is bad luck to ask a fisherman where he is going or say the words "good luck." It's not good to count the miles sailed or the miles left to reach port, and looking back at port soon after leaving the dock will bring bad luck.

Hearing church bells while at sea means someone on board will die. If the rim of a glass rings while on board, it must be stopped immediately or there will be a shipwreck. Never turn a boat counterclockwise, for it's believed to be turning the craft toward the Devil. If you wear the clothes of a dead sailor during the same voyage, it will curse the entire ship.

Another sign of bad luck and an omen of disaster on a fishing boat is to have bananas on board. This superstition comes from the 1700s, when boats with bananas as cargo ran aground, disappeared at sea, or lost their crews to a strange and deadly sickness. One cause was attributed to the lethal bites of tarantula spiders, which were brought aboard with the cargo.

Flowers on board are bad luck, representing a funeral wreath for the soon-to-be-doomed crew, and a shark following a ship is another sign of death. Some captains return to port if they find a rabbit, or rabbit skin, on board.

It is very bad luck to change the name of a boat once it has been launched, and boats whose name ends in the letter "a" will experience misfortune. Eyes painted on the bow of a ship help her to see her way safely through difficult conditions, but if you sight a comet it means someone on board is going to die.

Whether you're a scoffer, a serious believer, or a casual follower of these mysterious examples of long-held advice makes little difference. Superstitions have been around for centuries, and even in our modern, high-tech society, everyone can agree they're here to stay. Most folks will admit that performing a quick ritual doesn't take much time when done "just in case," or "to be sure." After all, when it comes to following superstitions, folks will often say, "It can't hurt."

Southern Maryland

IF RESIDENTS IN THE COUNTIES OF ST. MARY'S, ANNE ARUNDEL, Calvert, Charles, and Prince George's had been able to have their way, they would have joined up with the Confederacy during the Civil War. But there are more than Civil War ghost tales in this region of the state. Of particular local pleasure and pride are sightings of a wild blue dog, the curse of a hermit witch, a haunted lighthouse, and the favorite dancing spot of the Devil.

'His name is Mudd!'

Over the years, books, newspaper articles, and websites have reported the possibility of ghostly events at the historic home of Dr. Samuel Mudd. More intriguing, however, is the fact that events surrounding the assassination of Abraham Lincoln are said to have originated the well-known phrase, "His name is Mudd!" This derogatory comment is used to indicate that others should look unfavorably upon a particular individual. Many believe the remark came into use after the injured assassin John Wilkes Booth sought medial attention at the home of Dr. Samuel Mudd, who set the escaping assassin's broken leg. Some reports state that Mudd was simply doing a good deed and did not know he was treating the killer of the president of the United States. Other information and statements at Mudd's trial link the doctor and Booth, suggesting the two were acquaintances and that a Confederate spy had introduced them previously. One report added that Booth had sent liquor and supplies to Mudd's home weeks before the injured man's arrival after the assassination.

Mudd denied knowing Booth and stated that he was unaware the injured man had been involved in the killing and conspiracy. But the Maryland doctor was arrested, convicted, and sent to prison, where he served four years of his life sentence at Fort Jefferson in the Dry Tortugas, near Key West, Florida. In 1869, Mudd, who worked as a doctor in the Fort Jefferson prison, was pardoned by President Andrew Johnson.

Like Booth, Mudd also was a Maryland native, born in 1833 on a large plantation in Charles County. He attended Georgetown College in Washington, D.C., and in 1854 transferred to the University of Maryland in Baltimore, where he studied medicine and surgery and graduated in 1856. The building where Mudd studied, Davidge Hall in Baltimore, is open to the public. Visitors are able to sit in the same seats in Chemical Hall, the first-floor amphitheater, where Mudd, as a student, attended lectures.

Graveyard Treasure

An ever-popular topic is one of long-lost buried treasure, and what is a safer, yet more frightening, place to search for hidden wealth than in a graveyard? To help treasure seekers locate the hoard, a mysterious light is said to appear in and near Glen Haven Memorial Park, located on Ritchie Highway in Glen Burnie. According to one long-repeated legend, the cemetery was once a farm. The former owner of the land buried a cache of money and immediately thereafter murdered the servant or slave who had provided assistance digging the hiding place—proof of the adage "Dead men tell no tales." It is said that a floating light appears to help indicate the location where the money may be found. The only catch is that the mysterious glow is visible only at night—a time when few people, even serious treasure seekers, want to roam among the tombstones of the dead and disturb their peaceful eternal rest.

Moll Dyer

Long-time residents in Maryland's St. Mary's County know about "Moll Dyer," and although centuries have passed since the woman's death, the historical society in Leonardtown displays a rock that is believed to be a tangible link with the region's most prominent eerie figure. Of course, as with all legends, the versions vary from teller to teller and among different written sources. But here is a summary of Moll's fascinating and troubling tale.

Centuries ago, in the late 1600s, Moll Dyer lived in an unsightly hut in the forest, away from townsfolk. She was a hermit—odd looking, old, not sociable, and downright scary. Being out of the ordinary, and those being superstitious times, the accepted and respected citizens didn't associate with the likes of Moll, and when bad things happened—such as a freak storm, ruined crops, unexplained deaths and accidents, or a dried-up cow—blaming Moll seemed to be a good idea.

Remember, these were times when nearly two dozen folks were executed for witchcraft in Salem, Massachusetts, and Maryland historical records indicate at least twelve cases where persons were accused of witchcraft. There also were similar witch trials held in Pennsylvania and Virginia.

So, to solve the community's problems, the respected locals decided to burn Moll out of her secluded home. They thought this would drive her from the area and cause her to reside elsewhere, where she could ruin someone else's crops and dry up other farmers' cows. In the middle of winter, on a horribly frigid and windy night, a group of men crept through the woods and set fire to Moll's dwelling. Escaping the flames, Moll fled into the forest and hid. The mob went back to town, thinking their problems with Moll were over. Several days passed, and there was no sign of the dreaded witch. But soon a young boy, who had been walking in the woods, came into town and reported finding Moll's dead, frozen body. She was kneeling beside a rock, with one hand raised, as if in a state of prayer. The dead witch's other hand rested on the small boulder.

As news spread of her discovery, the townsfolk were relieved, initially. But then unexplained events and bad luck returned to the area. Animals died and there were sudden, fierce storms. Floods

and illness seemed to take up residence in St. Mary's County. It was as if Moll Dyer had cursed her attackers and all the other residents.

Then someone noticed an imprint on the boulder upon which the witch's corpse had been resting when her body had been found. And the mark seemed to be an impression of a handprint in the stone, as if Moll had died praying that the curse she directed upon her killers would remind the town of her power and their murderous deed.

Over time, the stream near her burned-out hut became known as Moll Dyer Run. Today Moll Dyer Road is another reminder of the area's resident witch.

Of course, nighttime travelers had reported seeing a ghostlike figure roaming the area. And there have been reports that on the coldest night of each year, the spirit of Moll returns to the area where her hut once stood and also to the rock upon which she died.

In the historical society booklet *Legends of St. Mary's: A Collection of Haunts, Witches and Other Strange Occurrences,* one chapter mentions that the famous rock was found and eventually moved on October 14, 1972, to the old jail in Leonardtown, which now houses the St. Mary's County Historical Society. Visitors are able to examine the 875-pound rock, which is located beside the old jail, and many try to locate and take pictures of the impression of Moll's hand and fingers.

Be aware, the Maryland Ghost and Spirit Association website states, "People report feeling uncomfortable around the rock." Cameras have malfunctioned, and some tourists have claimed they have experienced aching sensations while standing near the rock.

According to the historical society's booklet, Moll Dyer is an "omen of evil," equivalent to hearing the cry of the Banshee or meeting with the White Lady. If one encountered Moll's spirit on a lonely road or in a dark place, it certainly would foretell of "dire calamities." But that's what people used to believe. Right? After all, who still believes in witchcraft, spells, and curses? We're too sophisticated. Correct?

Maybe. But how many educated folks feel comfortable walking under a ladder, opening an umbrella in the house, or even walking near a black cat? Maybe the legend and curse of Moll Dyer and her periodic appearances aren't so unbelievable after all.

Devil's Ball Yard

During the War of 1812, the Chesapeake Bay was a watery battle-ground, with major engagements and scores of minor skirmishes between American and British sailors in crafts of all sizes. Admiral Cockburn and his deadly Rangers terrorized the villages along the Chesapeake coast, burning some to the ground and threatening others with attack from both his ships' cannons and his deadly landing parties.

While blockading the Chesapeake Bay and Potomac River that led to (then) Washington City, the British used the island of St. George—off St. Mary's County in the southern portion of the Potomac River—as a cemetery. British sailors of all ranks who perished while fighting in America were buried on the island, and to this day their graves remain scattered throughout the area. According to an article in the April 5, 1866, issue of the *St. Mary's Gazette,* a fair number of British bodies were buried in an area known as the Devil's Ball Yard.

The site was described as a "bald piece of ground, circular in form, about twenty feet in diameter, and entirely destitute of vegetation; not a blade of grass grew upon it till the late war was waged upon the Southern States." The earth's surface at this eerie site was smooth and circular. This occurred over time because the Devil visited the site each month, under cover of darkness, and held an informal ball, with much music, dancing, and drinking. But when the Civil War broke out, the king of the demons had so much pressing business to attend to, what with gathering up despondent souls, that he paused from his monthly revelry and stayed focused on his primary business—filling up the chambers of hell. The news article stated, the Devil "had so much business thrown upon his hand as to leave him no leisure to amuse himself."

Locals who dared visit the barren site returned with reports that no wood, weeds, or brush would ever grow in the confines of the demon's circle. "Such is the horror inspired by this place," the *Gazette* reported, "that but few care to pass near it after dark for fear of meeting with an adventure so terrifying that they might not return or be speechless for the rest of their days."

One Bay oysterman who took refuge on the island later reported an experience involving the sudden, unnatural appearance of a fog-shrouded wooden ship of sail. After embarking in complete silence, its phantom crew lured the mortal seaman to the haunted, barren spot. While there, the weary and fearful sailor witnessed serious drinking, violent dancing, and agitated playing of the fiddle (that being the well-known, favorite instrument of the Devil). When he awoke the next morning, with horrible aches throughout his body, the terrified sailor swore it was the Devil and his crew that had been celebrating on St. George Island the previous night. And the king of the demons said he would eventually meet the Chesapeake sailor one more time—at the gates of the Devil's permanent home.

Goatman of Prince George's County

The Beltsville Agricultural Research Center (BARC) is the largest area of undeveloped open space near Washington, D.C. The sixty-six hundred acres is administered by the Department of Agriculture, and much of the historic research site is off-limits to the public. But in one of its hidden, probably underground, high-tech laboratories, some believe, is the birthplace of the Goatman.

Motorists driving along the Baltimore-Washington Parkway and nearby roads enjoy BARC's rural landscape, featuring forests and historic farm buildings that offer a fleeting glimpse into the area's long-disappeared past. But no tourists, and only a small percentage of locals, are aware that while hiking BARC's trails or passing through wooded sections of the reservation, one might come face-to-face with the infamous legendary creature—Goatman.

Prince George's County's monster has been described as a white-colored, half-human, half-animal creature with goat hooves, a narrow face, and circular horns. Sometimes the monster runs on all fours; other times it races upright. It has also been said to resemble drawings of ancient Greek and Roman gods, playing a flute, but it has been seen more often wielding a deadly ax.

Goatman seems comfortable roaming BARC's deserted sections, and occasionally the creature has been known to interrupt the romantic activities of lovers inside cars parked in secluded wooded groves. More infrequently, Goatman has wandered off the reservation and taken mini trips into nearby towns, such as Greenbelt, Laurel, Bowie, and even College Park; the last site is home of the University of Maryland.

Homeowners have reported a strange creature roaming through their yards. Pet owners have attributed dog and cat deaths to the monster. Drivers have said they've seen a mysterious creature crossing the highway, racing across their headlight beams, and some residents even have claimed the creature has chased them.

According to legend, a scientist performing research on goats created the monster at BARC. Because of an accident during his experiments, the researcher turned into the half-man, half-goat creature. The mishap was hushed up, and authorities locked the mad scientist away. Sightings occur only when Goatman escapes, and this happens when he has been let out of his locked pen for exercise. Because he cannot exist in civilized society for long periods of time, Goatman always returns to his cell, located in a hidden chamber at BARC. A second version suggests that a goat, undergoing experimentation, was transformed into Goatman and killed the scientist conducting the research. Who's to know how much is true, how much is imagination, and how much is what the teller wants it to be?

But for those who intend to search for Goatman, keep in mind that most of the BARC facility is restricted, and many sections are closed off by tall fences. According to a 2001 report entitled "Public Health Assessment, Beltsville Agricultural Research Center, Beltsville, Prince George's County, Maryland," BARC originated as a 475-acre farm in Beltsville and was purchased by the USDA in 1910. It grew in size during the 1920s and '30s, eventually peaking at twelve thousand acres. Today, the property includes fields, pastures, orchards, forests, animal facilities, and nearly eight hundred structures, ranging from office buildings, laboratories, and greenhouses to shops and barns. Originally, BARC was named the Experiment Farm of the Dairy and Animal Husbandry Divisions; later it included the Bureau of Plant Industry and a variety of agencies involved in space exploration, environmental protection, and food and drug enforcement.

Over the years, contaminated areas have been identified at BARC, resulting, according to the 2001 Public Health Assessment, "from the handling and disposal of chemicals, including pesticides and radioactive agents, used in research and other activities conducted at the facility. Sources of contamination include landfills and dump sites, chemical storage areas, chemical burial sites, a burial site for material contaminated with low levels of radiation, and pesticide and herbicide mixing, application, and wash down areas. When pesticides or herbicides are sprayed on the site, warning signs are posted nearby, in accordance with the Federal Insecticide, Fungicide, and Rodenticide Act." Additional details in the report relate to areas of groundwater contamination.

After reading about BARC's large geographical size and its numerous sources of contamination and areas of concern, one might conclude that this restricted government complex provides ample habitat for the Goatman to live, thrive, hide, and even breed. Perhaps the theories about the possible origin and existence of Prince George's Goatman aren't too far off.

Blue Dog Ghost

Dogs, particularly black dogs, have been associated with folklore and local superstitions for centuries. The sudden appearances have predicted a wide range of positive and negative events, from impending dangerous weather and the location of undiscovered murder victims to the site of long-lost buried treasure.

The well-known ghost dog in Maryland has a slight variation because it's not black—but blue. Known as the "Ghostly Blue Dog" or "Blue Dog Ghost," its story has been circulated around the area of Port Tobacco in Charles County for more that several hundred years. In addition to the tale, the small town's history makes it a perfect setting for a ghostly story. Established in 1634, the village is on the site of an Indian village, was an area sympathetic to the Confederacy during the Civil War, and was part of John Wilkes Booth's escape route after he assassinated President Abraham Lincoln. However, it is the continued interest of ghost hunters in capturing a photo of the Blue Dog Ghost that has made Port Tobacco a paranormal hot spot.

In September 1962, a story in the *Baltimore American* newspaper featured an interview with George W. Hubley Jr., then director of the State Department of Economic Development. Mr. Hubley referred to Port Tobacco as the oldest ghost town in the United States, and he added that the Blue Dog was probably the oldest ghost in America. The article described the Blue Dog Ghost as the source of dozens of stories, rhymes, and ballads and stated that the creature "lives on in word-of-mouth tales, affectionately repeated. This makes him a genuine folk personality in an age of skepticism. He was a dog who died defending his master. That is all that is certainly known." But where certainty ends, the art of creative storytelling takes flight, and various versions of the story have been spun.

In the Baltimore reporter's account, the tale goes back to 1658, during Port Tobacco's shipbuilding and seaport days when the village had taverns, churches, and public government buildings. While the date and day are unknown, the month of the tragic incident was February.

It was a cold night when the dog's master, a traveling peddler carrying his sack, arrived in Port Tobacco. After drinking a bit too much in a local tavern, his loose lips spilled details about the wealth he was carrying in a money belt tied tightly about his waist. When the tipsy stranger was pressed by the crowd to prove his claims, the inebriated peddler removed the belt and showed off his gold to the crowd—certainly making an impressive but short-lived impression. After the pub's closing time, while stumbling up Rose Hill Road, not far from the tavern, the stranger was attacked and murdered. His faithful dog died fighting by his side, trying to protect his owner.

As proof, however, that folktales change over time, the website entitled Our Cities & Towns, featuring Charles County and Port Tobacco, refers to the event happening sometime after the Revolutionary War, more than one hundred years later than the first account. In this version, a soldier was returning home with his dog when they were attacked and killed by a Port Tobacco resident, who wanted gold and the deed to the soldier's estate. The murderer buried the gold and deed under a tree along Rose Hill Road. When he came back to dig up his stolen cache, the Blue Dog Ghost ran the murderer off, and he soon died of an unexplained illness. To this day, the dog still protects his master and his gold.

Whether you like the first or second version or one of the others that you will certainly run across, most folks agree—or want to believe—that the Blue Dog Ghost returns each year in February. And you have the best chance of meeting the phantom protector if you accidentally roam too close to the site of its slain master's unmarked grave and stolen gold—wherever that may be.

America's Most Haunted Lighthouse

Point Lookout Light stands at the southern tip of St. Mary's County. The structure was built in 1830, and it is one of the remaining lighthouses easily accessible to photographers along the Chesapeake Bay. Because of its long history, isolated location, and association with the Civil War Prison Camp that stood nearby, the beacon has frequently been called "America's Most Haunted Lighthouse."

In his book *Lighthouses of Maryland and Virginia: History, Mystery, Legends and Lore,* author Bob Trapani Jr. described the site in this way: "There is no other Chesapeake Bay Lighthouse, and arguably none other in America, which possesses such a connection to grisly suffering and death—all of which occurred directly below its lifesaving beam—than Point Lookout Lighthouse. In fact, the light station's history is littered with unfavorable circumstances, seemingly bad luck, and unexplained mystery."

The first keeper died suddenly only two months after taking over his post. A subsequent keeper's cat contaminated the oil and broke more than two dozen lamps, causing the keeper to be denied his pay for a full year. But the biggest impact to the light and its keepers occurred immediately after the Battle of Gettysburg, when ten thousand Rebel prisoners were deposited at the peninsula—suddenly transformed into a prison—surrounding the light. In the coming months and years, misery, disease, and death would increase to epidemic levels, as more than fifty-five thousand prisoners would be sent to Point Lookout and more than thirty-five hundred of these soldiers would die.

After the Civil War, in October 1878, the steamer *Express* sank in the bay off of Point Lookout. A ship's officer named Joseph Haney is said to have attempted to row to shore to gain assistance from the lighthouse keeper, but because of the raging storm he never made it to Point Lookout. Haney's corpse washed up along the shore a few days later, and he was buried in the immediate area. A former resident of the lighthouse reported seeing a man at the back porch, wearing clothes from a historic period and looking as if he was distressed. When this person opened the door, the figure floated across the lawn and disappeared toward the Bay. Perhaps it was the confused spirit of Mr. Haney, trapped in another dimension because of his sudden and violent death.

Once the Navy, and subsequently the state of Maryland, took possession of the lighthouse and rehabilitated it, former tenants of the lighthouse began reporting their experiences of unexplained voices, sightings, and other phenomena. Gerald (Gerry) J. Sword, a state park official who had lived in the lighthouse, made a list of unexplained experiences. Many of his stories are included in considerable detail in the county historical society's book *Legends of St. Mary's*. His personal stories are associated with crashing objects, a glowing wall, snoring sounds, voices and footsteps in the hallway and on the stairs, strong odors, lights turning on and off, doors banging shut, and his dog reacting to apparently unseen activity.

Noted paranormal investigator Dr. Hans Holzer visited the light with several associates, including Nancy Stallings, a medium with the Maryland Committee for Psychical Research. Photographer Ron Stallings captured a photo in 1980 of what appears to be an apparition of a Confederate soldier leaning against a wall in a second-floor bedroom on the Potomac side of the building.

Laura Berg was the last tenant to live in the lighthouse building from 1979 to 1981. She reported a number of strange experiences, including hearing someone walking in the hallway outside her bedroom door and noticing strong smells. Visitors at the light during Laura's residency reported hearing whispered voices and seeing apparitions. She returns periodically to conduct tours and paranormal investigations and to encourage restoration efforts with Robert Hall of the Paranormal Research Society of North America. Laura has been featured in numerous articles and programs. A detailed account of her experiences, the history of the lighthouse, modern and historic photographs, restoration efforts—along with séances and psychic investigations held at the lighthouse—can be found at www.ptlookoutlighthouse.com.

Laura said activity at Point Lookout is nothing new. She said they have found reports of people speaking of unusual experiences back more than a half century, in the 1940s. Despite the unsettling events that sometimes occurred at Point Lookout, when asked what it was like to live in the lighthouse with its truly magnificent view of the lower Chesapeake Bay, Laura said, without hesitation, "Every day was a blessing."

Laura now resides in Baltimore. But based on two and one-half years of living in the lighthouse and conducting investigations since, when asked if Point Lookout Lighthouse is haunted, she answered: "Yes. I have no doubt that there are multiple spirits haunting this lighthouse."

Another strange incident was mentioned in the book *Phantom in the Bedchamber*. A park ranger reported the incident that occurred along MD Route 5, which travels through Point Lookout State Park and ends at the main entrance to the lighthouse, or "the point area," as the spot is called. This tip of land, surrounded on three sides by water, has an eight-foot-high chain-link fence that encloses the lighthouse. The entire restricted area is off-limits to the public, because the U.S. Navy operates a radar tracking facility just a few yards away from the lighthouse.

One evening at the point area, a young couple in a Jeep Wrangler stopped the ranger as they were heading north away from the point, about one hundred feet from the lighthouse. After flagging down the ranger, the Jeep's driver reported that his girlfriend had seen someone patrolling the lighthouse area, inside the fence line.

She said, "I swear, I saw someone inside the fence, close to the lighthouse, just a few minutes ago. He was wearing a dark uniform and had a small flat hat, and was pacing back and forth. He was carrying a long rifle on his shoulder with a long knife sticking off the top of the gun."

The ranger said no one was permitted inside the fenced area, but he also realized the young woman had accurately described a Civil War soldier on guard duty. He told the young woman, "You are not the first person to report seeing a possible ghost, and I'll add this to my list of stories."

In the introduction of that book, *Washington Post* writer David Montgomery indicated that development, and I would add the word "neglect," is a major threat to haunted sites. Doing their best to protect the structure, spirits, and stories, Laura Berg and Robert Hall recently formed the nonprofit Point Lookout Lighthouse Preservation Society Inc. (PLLPS). To preserve the history, buildings, and land of Point Lookout Lighthouse, the group hosts monthly open houses and paranormal investigation events in the mild weather months.

In 1998, the Learning Channel included a segment at Point Lookout on its program *Haunted Lighthouses*. George Steitz, writer and producer of several other television documentaries, including

Ghost Waters, made several visits to Point Lookout during the film-
ing. "Lighthouses," he said, "are romantic and spiritual places.
They evoke a sense of history, especially in America, where they
seem to be our answer to Europe's castles."

But are any of them haunted?

"I did not see or hear any ghosts myself," Steitz said. "The closest I came to a supernatural experience was a strange and unsettling feeling I had at Point Lookout Lighthouse. I can't explain it
because I don't think we have words to accurately describe this
type of experience. At another location someone once commented
that in certain places there may be rips or holes in time through
which we can sense activity in another dimension, one inhabited
by what we call ghosts. I thought about this at Point Lookout. It
may in fact be a genuinely haunted lighthouse."

Western Maryland

MARYLAND'S WESTERN COUNTIES ARE GARRETT, ALLEGHENY, Frederick, and Washington. This section of Maryland is home to its most famous monster, the Snallygaster, which has been known to take flight and visit other sections of the state. The area also features many other rural ghost stories and superstitions reflecting the culture of the early settlers, as well as tales about historic battles in the region.

Phantom Flutist

There's a floating melody that travels through the wooded hillsides of northwest Maryland, near the town of Emmitsburg. Most pass off the snatches of a high-pitched melody as the swirling wind. Others claim it's the screeching of night owls or some disturbed forest creatures. But long-time locals know the real source—it's the ghost.

Larry Dielman is his name, and playing the flute is his game. That's the answer that has been given since the tale began in 1884, soon after the first tune took wind, but that's the middle of our story. It is best that we start at the beginning.

According to word-of-mouth tales and articles in the *Emmitsburg Chronicle* (as early as 1884) and the *Baltimore Sun* (as recent as 2001), the kindly tale begins with Professor Casper Dielman, a German musician of some note who came to America in the early

1800s. After composing inaugural marches for four U.S. presidents and directing orchestras in New York City, Philadelphia, and Baltimore, the accomplished musician arrived at Mount Saint Mary's College in 1834, to enjoy nature and mold young musical minds.

In 1838, a son Larry was born. The younger Dielman eventually received some musical training and soon enjoyed playing a number of instruments at the side of his father, but the son was somewhat of a musical disappointment. Apparently he never took his musical talents to new heights, instead being content to use it in a playful way to attract the attention of the ladies and entertain his friends.

Larry became a grocer, married the love of his life, and seemed to have a perfect existence—for a time—until his bride ran off and left him to endure a solitary life. Neighbors recall a picture of Larry as an older, lonely man, alone on his store's front porch singing aloud of his lost love.

In the early 1880s, the old professor died. That following Christmas, Larry walked to his father's grave, stood above the stone, and lifted a flute to his lips. People in the nearby town recalled hearing the shrill strains of a lamented melody. The song was "When Glory Lit the Midnight Air," a song composed by Larry's recently deceased father. In response, the locals wrapped themselves in winter garb and walked to the gravesite, located near the Grotto of Our Lady of Lourdes. In silence, they witnessed the musical expression of a lonely son's special love.

As years passed, the event became an annual tradition, with Larry leading a small procession up the steep hill to stand beside his father's gravesite. In coming years, the tradition changed slightly, with the musical tribute occurring on Christmas Eve. As Larry grew older and he was unable to make the climb, friends placed his frail body onto a sled and pulled him up the hill so he could continue to perform.

One version of the story states that in 1923 Larry Dielman died, along with the tradition. A more eerie rendition of the tale, written by Frederick N. Rasmussen for the *Baltimore Sun*, suggests that despite the most bone-chilling temperatures and falling snow or sleet, Larry never missed a Christmas performance. But his last, in 1922, will be remembered most. "Townspeople heard the notes from his flute," Rasmussen wrote, "which then abruptly stopped.

He was found unconscious in the snow and died the following spring. He was buried in a plot next to his father." So ended a musical family's custom that had developed into an anticipated local event, but others claimed this was not the case.

In an *Emmitsburg Chronicle* article published in the late 1800s, the unknown author wrote, "Old-timers say that if you listen very carefully on Christmas Eve or Christmas morning, you can still hear the ethereal strains of beautiful flute music floating down from the cemetery. A short time later, it is gone, not to be heard again for another year."

Gravity Hill and Spook Hill

Spook Hill, or Gravity Hill as it is sometimes called, is said to exist in the area of Burkittsville. Some say the legendary location is closer to Frederick. Others will direct ghost hunters and interested parties to locations between Sharpsburg and Antietam. There is even a listing of a Gravity Hill near Baltimore, plus numerous other sites around the country.

In each case, the essence of this well-known tale is the same: Stop your car and shut off the engine at a specific spot in the road. Place the gearshift in neutral, exit the vehicle, and watch in amazement as your empty car moves mysteriously "up" the hill, apparently on its own power, or with a little bit of unseen help.

The logical explanation is that you are experiencing an optical illusion and the auto is actually heading downhill. But the more interesting, paranormal reasons for this supernatural occurrence depend upon several factors, including the teller, the time of the occurrence, and any tragic or historical events that took place at the particular haunted "Spook Hill" site.

Outside Burkittsville, between Frederick, Maryland, and Harpers Ferry, West Virginia, the cause is placed on the apparently bored and restless shoulders of invisible, and ever-present, Civil War soldiers. One report claims the historic events occurred during the Battle of South Mountain, but others credit the Battle of Antietam (or Sharpsburg). In both instances, the ghosts of desperate Civil War soldiers—in one instance Union, in another tale Confederate—have been seen in the area pushing phantom cannons into position to try to turn the tide of the deadly battle. During their efforts these men were killed, but they have remained, still trying to resolve their unfinished business.

Some ghost-hunting visitors have even tried to prove that the spectral artillerists are pushing their automobiles. One evidence-securing technique is to place a layer of white powder on the rear car bumper and inspect the area for indications of finger or hand marks after the car stops moving. (For those interested in visiting Spook Hill near Burkittsville, ask the locals for directions to the site, which is said to be on Gapland Road.)

Washington County Folk Medicine and Superstitions

It is amazing what you can find in the bowels of the newspaper archives. As if waiting for my arrival, the article "Maryland Superstitions: Sign of a Crowing Hen—Bad Luck To Move Parsley," from a May 1898 issue of the *Baltimore Sun* newspaper, literally fell into my lap. The unnamed reporter prefaced the piece, stating, "The curious beliefs still prevailing in some parts of Washington County, Md., are noteworthy." Among them were a number of interesting vignettes, which are summarized below.

Farmers believed that the crowing of a hen foretold the impending death of a family member, and that the fowl should be killed immediately to break the spell of soon-to-arrive, deadly bad luck. While mentioning this belief to a young lady, the reporter wrote that the woman had replied she would have done so herself, based on what had happened to her mother years earlier.

As the story goes, the mother's sister owned a pet hen, which she loved very much. "One day, while the child was seated in a rocking chair, the fowl hopped in her lap and crowed. Owing to the fondness of the child for the hen, its life was spared, but the little girl herself died within six months. This would indicate a specific reason for the adage that 'crowing hens should have their heads chopped off.'"

Numerous signs were believed to predict the coming of the Grim Reaper, such as the blossoming of a fruit tree a second time in the summer, hearing the unison sound of two church bells chiming, and the chirp of the plaintive whip-poor-will beside a door. Of a less threatening nature, to move a parsley plant was considered bad luck, but some thought to even plant parsley would bring ill fortune. Taking a small egg called a "pullet's egg" or "bad luck egg" and throwing it over the house could solve the hex. The resulting broken egg was said to cancel the bad luck.

A rather unusual practice would cure a case of the fits. Take a live chicken and plunge it—feathers, protestations, and all—into a pot of boiling water. Cook at that high temperature for several hours and give a cup of the resulting murky broth to the patient. A variation of the cure is applied externally. Take a completely black-feathered chicken, split the fowl down the middle, and bind it to the bare breast of the afflicted person. (A few hours of that should settle the agitated patient down real fast.)

The next unusual story occurred along a highway near Hagerstown, when a couple was leading a colt to sell at market. Somehow the animal tore its hoof and was bleeding severely. "Stopping at a farmhouse on the way for help," the reporter wrote, "the mistress thereof informed the travelers that she could stop the bleeding and getting her Bible she read a certain verse over the colt's head and the hemorrhage ceased. While speaking of this to a Hagerstown lady . . . she told me her husband had precisely the same experience with a colt, only in the last case the accident had occurred in a field and it was the doctor whom they called on who in this case read the verse."

Another story took place in Hancock, where a couple that believed in witches hoped to solve their problem by asking a druggist for medicine to take a spell off the wife, but the article does not tell whether he was successful in obtaining the cure. However, near Millstone, a man who had quarreled with his neighbor had more satisfying results. He "filled a four-ounce bottle with water and buried it: remarking 'When the bottle is empty, my neighbor will be dead.' The neighbor died in four months. The bottle was dug up and there was not a drop of water in it."

Garrett County's Ghost Towns

The term "ghost town" is most often associated with the Wild West, where empty buildings and the remnants of old foundations are scattered in clusters throughout the desert. The settlement names on old maps no longer show any sign of life. No townsfolk walk deserted streets. No commerce takes place in boarded-up stores. No church bells peal, calling faithful congregations to worship. Instead, the remaining buildings offer curious visitors a hint of their long-gone glory. Of course, some believe these scarred walls and caved roofs contain lingering memories of the ghosts of souls of what had been, but will never be again.

But there are ghost towns in the eastern part of the country. My first encounter with such an Atlantic Coast site was near Chincoteague, Virginia. A rugged crab pot maker suggested I drive up to Franklin City and see the "old ghost town." The village had been a ferry terminal that was used to transport people and supplies bound for Chincoteague Island. It was a busy spot until the modern road was built across the marshland connecting the fishing village, famous for the Assateague ponies and the annual roundup, with the mainland. Now Franklin City is off the beaten track and draws little attention and fewer visitors.

There also was a village and businesses on Assateague Island, but they were abandoned in the 1930s when the federal government bought the land. Today, Chincoteague National Wildlife Refuge is a popular destination, and few tourists are aware of the early fishing villages and settlements that thrived on the barrier island.

Ghost towns also exist in the northwestern section of Maryland. Most of these hamlets were mining, logging, or industrial towns that were active in the late 1800s and early 1900s, and some continued until the mid-twentieth century. Eventually, these communities became victims of progress. As the natural resources were played out or demand for coal and timber decreased, the towns' reasons for being disappeared, and so did the people who lived there.

In *Ghost Towns of the Upper Potomac,* a book compiled by the Garrett County Historical Society, photographs and short stories spotlight the small mining and logging villages that once existed along the north branch of the Potomac River in Maryland and West Virginia from Fairfax to Bloomington.

Readers will learn how the railroad followed the resources, bringing people to create the villages and then hauling the ore and timber to large city markets. Train stations, fire companies, village centers, town halls, banks, post offices, general stores, theaters, hotels, and churches catered to the needs of these rugged residents and traveling salesmen. Of course, not far from the dirt streets, bordered by rows of cookie-cutter-style mine workers' houses, were the cemeteries, which still remain, although some have been reclaimed by the hillsides.

And the town names—Kitzmiller, Vindex, Shaw, Bloomington, Dodson, Shallmar, Kempton, Gorman, Deer Park, Louise, and Steyer—are as colorful as the mining operations themselves: Grafton Mining Company, Dean Coal Company, Western Maryland Coal Company, Three Fork Coal Company, Pee Wee Coal Company, Jaffy Coal Company. And the place names such as Dill Hole, Wolf Den Run, Lost Land Run, Deep Run, and Three Fork Run complement the color and history of the operations and their towns.

In the introduction of *Ghost Towns of the Upper Potomac*, the authors acknowledge that their book is not a complete history of the region, but written "to give some insight into the people and towns which existed." But they also caution explorers that only a few of the towns still remain and can be visited by automobile. Many others can be found and accessed only by hiking through brush, heading down horse trails, and following the tracks of the old Western Maryland Railway.

Those who persist in their search will be rewarded with the sites of old foundations, crumbling structures, long-forgotten tombstones, and ruins of former bridges and mining operations. But surely, among these long-vacant sites—where so many worked and lived, and later died and were placed to rest—there's a chance that some remnant of their human spirit might have remained behind. Perhaps.

Old Braddock Treasure

In the 1830s, an inn stood at the settlement of Old Braddock, which is located west of Frederick, approximately where the road splits, diving Route 40 with Alternate Route 40.

This main highway was an extension of the Old Cumberland Road, which led to Baltimore, and it was well traveled by both area residents and commercial haulers. According to local lore, the inn was well known as a drinking spot where fellow haulers could stop to share tales and catch up on news while downing many a glass of brew. Quite often these raucous sessions extended into the wee hours of the morning. Whether the principal in our story was a guest at the inn or a teamster driving his rig, no one is sure. But the tale that has been handed down is well known and varies little.

For unknown reasons, an unnamed traveler or driver buried a chest of gold and jewels near the Old Braddock area tavern, or along a nearby mountainside, and headed off. Two years later, when he returned to dig up his hidden wealth, he was fatally injured during a sudden mountain storm. The tavern keeper came to the traveler's aid, but the stranger's injuries were fatal. While dying, the visitor told the innkeeper about the buried jewels, which he had hidden for safekeeping in the nearby area, and he said they had been stolen from European royalty. Unfortunately for the well-intentioned innkeeper, the stranger died before sharing the treasure's exact location.

Without success, the innkeeper spent the next several years digging up the area near his tavern. Some believe the lost chest remains, waiting to be found by a persistent and lucky treasure hunter. The only clues are that it rests on a hillside or near a long-gone tavern, somewhere within eyesight of the split in the Old National Road, west of Frederick.

General Braddock's Gold

In Allegheny County, near Frostburg, a state of Maryland historical marker states: "General Braddock's 2nd camp on the march to Fort Duquesne June 14th, 15th, 1755. The old Braddock Road passed to the southeast of the National Road from Clarysville to the 'Shades of Death' near 'Two Mile Run.' The National Road was begun by the Government in 1811."

The sketchy reference makes note of the passing of troops led by British Major General Edward Braddock during the French and Indian War. Unfortunately, Braddock was the victim of poor planning and little accurate information of what he was up against. The general set out from Maryland with several thousand men—plus all their supplies, food, and several pieces of heavy artillery. He was heading to Fort Duquesne, located near what is today Pittsburgh, Pennsylvania. Braddock's mission was to battle the French.

The British general's map indicated the location of several rivers he was prepared to cross, but the diagrams left out the mountains, cliffs, and swamps. The commander also had not planned on surprise attacks by hostile Indians, thick brush and forests, lack of roads, wild animals, swarms of insects, and the intense summer humidity. In order to move his large guns, Braddock's Irish and Scottish troops spent considerable time and energy chopping away brambles and cutting trees to widen the Indian trails he was following to accommodate his weary column of slow-moving troops and supplies.

Certainly Braddock's March was anything but a success. However, it's believed that the general had brought along sufficient amounts of gold, which he planned to use to purchase supplies from farmers and villagers along the route. Those who survived his march claim that Braddock ordered the gold buried when he was under fire or worried about an impending attack.

No one knows the location of his treasure, since Braddock never shared the secret before he was mortally wounded at the Battle of Monongahela on July 9, 1755. He died within a week on July 13, 1775, and ghost hunters have circulated reports of sightings of the general's ghost near his grave. But his spirit also has been reported in the mountains of Allegheny County, where some suggest he's seeking the gold he left behind.

Treasure hunters say the best places to start hunting for the riches are near historical markers mentioning Braddock or his march, like the one in Cumberland that states: "The National Road (called The Cumberland Road) . . ." is part of the "route of 'Braddock's Road,' which followed 'Nemacolin's Path,' an Indian trail, over which George Washington traveled in 1754 to Fort LeBoeuf." But since Braddock's name is featured on a fair number of historic plaques in Garrett and Montgomery counties in Maryland, as well as on others in Pennsylvania and Virginia, there are plenty of places to search.

Ghosts of Wise's Well

Disposing of bodies left on a Civil War battlefield was a difficult and disturbing task that had to be handled. Sometimes fellow soldiers placed comrades in hastily dug, shallow graves near the killing fields. When opposing troops left battle areas quickly, local farmers and townsfolk buried those left behind, often performing brief and informal ceremonies over both Union and Confederate soldiers. And on some occasions, the government hired area residents to bury the corpses, many of them young men who died far from their homes.

A grisly legend is associated with an engagement that was part of the much larger Battle of South Mountain. It occurred in 1862, in the western part of the state between Frederick and Hagerstown, near the site of the Reno Monument. The marker indicates the spot where Major General Jesse Lee Reno, commander of a group of Union volunteers, was killed at a site known as Fox's Gap. Nearby in an old cabin lived Daniel Wise and his family; they wisely fled the area during the battle but returned to find their property littered with the bodies of dead soldiers from both sides.

At this point, the legend takes a fork in the road. In one version, a Union burial detail was at the Wise homestead and had buried their comrades in graves around the family cabin. However, the Yanks had dumped nearly five dozen Rebels down the Wise family well. Afterwards, the ghosts of the restless spirits haunted Wise and others who came near their inappropriate burial site.

Another explanation has the Union Army paying Wise five dollars for every soldier he buried following the Battle of South Mountain. To make the most of the government's generous offer, it's said that Wise, without proper ceremony, tossed about fifty dead soldiers into a nearby dry well that was no longer used by the family.

Soon afterwards, the disrespected spirits began to haunt anyone passing the area near the well. But of more concern to Wise, some of the soldiers' ghosts visited the greedy old man in his sleep, and they promised to haunt him forever. To break the hex, the troubled farmer had two options: move away or provide the bodies with their expected—and paid for—decent burial. Wise wisely selected the latter choice, and somehow he retrieved the bodies of the troubled ghost soldiers from his dry well and gave them a more respectful sendoff.

Taking a moment to think a bit beyond the basic facts of this legend, one can only imagine the horrifying task that awaited Old Man Wise. For to accomplish this job, he had to lower himself into a deep cavern, gather up decaying body parts, and fight off the stench and horrifying sights that attacked all his senses. After he was well into this effort, there were times when he probably wished he had selected the first option and moved away, leaving the restless spirits to roam at will. Of course, he could have avoided most of his troubles by fulfilling the original terms of the deal, but he succumbed to human nature's tendency to make a quick buck and eventually paid the price in full, and then some.

Snallygaster

When the German immigrants arrived in western Maryland and Pennsylvania, they brought along more of the Old Country culture than just food, language, dances, and costumes. They also brought along their monsters. Among the most distinctive creatures to settle in and hide among the wooded niches of America's eastern hills and valleys is the Snallygaster—a fearsome, dragonlike flying beast—described as having a very long (up to twenty-five-foot) wingspan, claws made of hot glowing metal, a long pointed beak, and a red blazing eye in the middle of its forehead.

The Snallygaster has been defined as a mythical dragonlike beast, with an acute sense of smell, and it dwells in the state of Maryland. The principal concentration of this rare animal is around Frederick County. It's believed that even Theodore Roosevelt hunted the beast, but Bully Teddy, also known as the Bull Moose, tended to hunt a lot of big game, and the Snallygaster is about as big as they come.

The original German name is *schnell geist,* roughly translated into "fast ghost" or "quick spirit," and this poltergeist has powers to move things around or cause unexplained noises and unpleasant smells. Snatching small, unattended children for feeding, terrifying travelers, and providing subject matter for a bored population and festival storytellers seem to be the creature's main claims to fame. Academic scholars have offered that the dragon creature is a combination of American Indian, Pennsylvania Dutch, and isolated mountain-man lore all rolled up into one.

An interesting coincidence comes up in the chapter "Of Snallygasters and Other Creatures" in Alyce T. Weinberg's book *Spirits of Frederick.* It occurred in the year 1735 when the creature seems to have migrated to the Middletown area along with German settlers. However, aficionados of the unexplained know that 1735 is the same year attributed to the birth of the infamous Jersey Devil, only two states and a quick evening flight away to the east. Is this simply a coincidence, or might the two dragonlike demon creatures be related in some way? Who's to know?

While the Jersey Devil has developed a national reputation—think New Jersey Devils, the professional hockey team; or the subject of episodes of the *X-Files;* or a featured character in the movie *Thirteenth Child: The Legend of the Jersey Devil, Volume I,* to offer only a few examples—the Snallygaster has been misinterpreted, misunderstood, and mistreated to the point of even being killed off.

In her book, Weinberg refers to Folger McKinsey, an editor of the *Frederick Daily News,* who ran a nine-part series in the 1950s on the mountain monster and then destroyed it by dropping it into a vat of moonshine mountain liquor, where it drowned. Despite the "reported" demise of the flying beast, stories of the Snallygaster carrying off small game, pets, chickens, and even people have been reported over the years. It was common for old-timers in Frederick County and points west and south to blame anything that wasn't explainable on the antics of the Snallygaster. But on one occasion, the beastly bird made the front page of a well-known national daily paper.

"Gorilla-like Beast Seen Roaming Woods Near Elkton—In Md.'s 'Snallygaster' Country" was the *Washington Post* page-one headline that hit the newsstands on August 28, 1953. The attention-grabbing, oversized type appeared one day after the small-town *Cecil Whig* front-page banner proclaimed: "Definite Possibility Large Monkey-like Animal Loose, Evidence Shows." It seemed the western Maryland monster was still alive and flying, and it had headed east, apparently searching for fresher game.

Today, more than fifty years later, there are still vivid recollections, spirited talk, and even some fond memories in Cecil County about the strange creature that was sighted but never captured. The primary incidents are said to have taken place in a wooded farming region, just south of the Maryland-Pennsylvania line, north of the Mendenhall Crossroads in the area of Blue Ball Road, close to Nellies Corner, Blake Road, and Lombardville. Of course, the countryside has changed quite a bit during the five decades since the sightings. Some of the old homesteads and outbuildings have been sold and torn down. Developers have placed modern homes on a good portion of the rolling farmland. The local post office and fam-

ily general stores have closed, and automobile traffic is more common than it was in the sleepy 1950s.

But remnants of the unsolved county mystery still exist. The low, block-like mushroom house, near the field where farmers H. S. Osborne and Ray "Brady" Potter reported that they sighted the hairy creature, still stands. And, perhaps more importantly, some of the actual participants in the Great Snallygaster Hunt are still around and eager to tell tales about their role in the grand search for Cecil County's Creature in the Cornfield.

According to a story by reporter Don Hanes in the August 27, 1953, issue of the *Cecil Whig:* "Rumors that a gorilla or some such animal is prowling Cecil County took on strong tones of authority this week when a Lombardville farmer told how he saw the beast from a distance of twenty feet on two occasions." Osborne reported that he had seen the creature the first time on August 12 at the edge of the cornfield only twenty feet away from his mushroom house near Lombardville. The farmer said the animal stood looking at him for "a second or two" and disappeared. It was about three o'clock in the afternoon, and the day was clear with good visibility. A week later, Osborne and farmer Ray "Brady" Potter saw the creature, which they described as being about six feet tall, standing erect, with a pink ring around its face and brownish hair. Searchers later found about twenty ears of corn, with their husks pulled back and partially eaten, scattered around a clearing in the woods.

A short time later, Joseph Eggers, who lived about a quarter mile from Osborne, was working on a chicken house. He reported hearing a dog barking and, upon looking up, he sighted a brownish, man-sized animal that took several steps and disappeared into a cornfield.

The *Whig* reported that calls to law enforcement authorities about a gorilla-like creature had been circulating throughout the county for about a month prior to these sightings. The sheriff's office had gotten about one hundred calls regarding a "prowling animal," and the game warden said his phone was "ringing constantly." When the Osborne and Eggers reports came in, officials started to think there actually might be some unusual creature roaming out and about.

A *Whig* reporter contacted Fred Ulmer, who was curator of mammals at the Philadelphia Zoo, and conducted an interview. He indicated that if there was a monkeylike animal in the vicinity, it probably wasn't a gorilla, because there were only two in Philadelphia and one in Baltimore. With replacement costs estimated at $50,000 each, there would have been quite an alarm if one of them had been found to be missing.

A chimpanzee was a possibility, since a full-grown chimp could reach a height of five feet. Worth only about $600, they are common in carnivals, and some are even kept as household pets. One might have escaped and be roaming the area. They could eat just about anything, including corn. However, they tend to travel and not stay in one spot. Sightings in the county indicated the beast was in the area for an extended period of time.

A Pennsylvania bear was another suggested possibility. "But," the *Whig* stated, "Osborne said he had seen bears and the beast he saw was not a bear."

The *Washington Post* article captured Osborne's and Potter's reactions to their joint sighting: "Osborne said he told Potter to watch it and ran for his shotgun. When he got to the door and looked back, Potter was right at his heels.

"'If you want it watched, watch it yourself,' Osborne quoted his friend. The animal was gone when they returned."

The *Whig* reported, "Rumors were wild and varied about the gorilla." They included a report that a gorilla had escaped from a boat at Chesapeake City and that another strange animal had jumped from a ship in the C & D Canal, but had gotten away after being shot at. One woman said she heard that a circus train going through the county had lost two black panthers and a gorilla, and someone reported seeing the beast on the porch of the Howard House Tavern.

Farmers were keeping their shotguns handy and were warning anyone stupid enough to be roaming around dressed in a monkey suit that the situation was nothing to be monkeying around with. Many residents were prepared to shoot on sight, and parents were keeping their children close to home.

According to the *Washington Post,* the area of the sightings is believed to be the haunt of the mythical Snallygaster, a flying sea monster believed to inhabit the Chesapeake Bay and other rural and secluded valleys to the west. A 1996 interview with several long-time Cecil County residents, who all lived within walking distance of the strange events and were in their teens at the time, produced some humorous comments and memories.

One resident recalled heading down Blue Ball Road on a usually quiet Sunday morning and coming upon a neighbor who was shooting a pistol in the air and shouting: "There's a gorilla running around loose!"

"I thought to myself, 'That's probably nothing but one of our crazy neighbors in a bear suit,'" the man remembered, but it didn't stop him and his neighbors from loading their weapons and heading out into the fields to track down whatever might be roaming about.

Phone lines were buzzing, loaded shotguns were kept at the ready, and landowners were patrolling their property. Sightings and rumors were the talk of the county, from Rising Sun to Chesapeake City, but particularly in the region near Lombardville, since that's where two farmers swore that they saw the gorilla-like beast. The sightings apparently generated official airplane surveillance, indicating area officials were taking the reports seriously.

Eventually, nothing was found, the excitement died down, and everyone assumed that the dragon flew off to the west, the gorilla returned to the circus, or the kids hid away their bear suit. But for a short time during one sleepy 1950s summer—thanks to the *Washington Post*'s inappropriate use of a colorful term, and the runaway imaginations of county residents—Maryland's Snallygaster flew east and terrorized Cecil County.

Mount's Troubled Spirits

Mount Saint Mary's College and Seminary rests on fourteen hundred acres in the Catoctin Mountains of Western Maryland. Founded in 1808, it is believed to be the second oldest Catholic institution of higher learning in the country. It also is said to be home of more than a few pesky ghosts, but this shouldn't prove surprising. After all, nearly every college campus boasts its share of school spirits. However, St. Mary's rural location—and its proximity to the Mason-Dixon Line and the famous Battle of Gettysburg—makes it an ideal site for more than a fair share of local lore.

The school's most famous phantom appears to be The Reverend Simon Brute, a former president of the college who died in 1839.

The long-cassock-wearing apparition has been reported to glide at a smooth and steady pace across the attractive campus, and the specter often offers a nod to passing students and faculty. Naturally, it's not surprising that he's believed to hang about in Brute Hall, a dormitory named in his honor. And some say this particular ghost's favorite haunt is Room 252.

One year, a visiting priest was assigned to the room. The cleric checked in, took a walk around the campus, and returned to find all of his belongings spread about, as if someone had tossed them in a fit of anger. Another priest, who owned a pet cat, was given the room, but he moved out after his pet began hissing at an unseen being and spent its time cowering beneath the bed.

In a 2002 Halloween article in the *Washington Post,* written by Linton Weeks, the reporter noted that students who had stayed in the room told of unexplained flushing toilets, flashing light switches, and changing stations on the television. Weeks also reported the tale associated with McCaffrey Hall, involving a slave named Leander, who had worked at the college in the 1880s. When Leander was accused of stealing, his left hand was severed, and according to legend, the limb was buried in the college quadrangle. Certainly, this tale is a gift for those interested in perpetuating creepy college tales, and Weeks's article adds, "To this day, residents of McCaffrey report seeing a severed hand here and there or hearing fingers scratching on dorm windows." No doubt, the troubled hand is seeking the rest of its body, and it is believed it will roam the campus until its search is over.

Witches and Witchcraft

Mention the word "witch" and Salem, Massachusetts, probably comes to mind. Certainly, the mass hysteria and public trials in 1692 branded Salem as the center of witchcraft in America. Today this New England town remains a tourist magnet, ensuring big business through historical witchcraft tours, occult souvenir shops, and special events based on a supernatural theme.

But there were other places in seventeenth- and eighteenth-century America where women, and sometimes men and children, were accused of possessing supernatural powers. Of course, they didn't have to do much to be branded as suspicious. Here are a few examples of what could cause you to end up on trial for your life: acting or appearing strange; talking to a farm animal or pet; riding a broomstick; using herbs to cure illness; speaking in a strange language; growing a good crop; having a bad crop; looking at your neighbor with ill intent; arguing with a well-respected citizen, especially a politician, landowner, or member of the clergy; avoiding contact with other villagers; and consorting with the Devil.

In *Historical Witches and Witchtrials in North America,* compiled by Marc Carlson, there are scores of instances of witchcraft accusations and trials. They occurred in New England, the Mid-Atlantic, the Deep South, and even the far Western territories. And while dunking, whipping, being burned at the stake, as well as being imprisoned and shunned are the more common punishments, the most unusual disposition of a witch occurred in Salem in 1692, when Giles Corey was pressed to death after refusing repeatedly to plead to accusations of witchcraft.

In the counties surrounding the Chesapeake Bay, there were a number of recorded cases of witchcraft. However, in 1999, publicity surrounding the movie *The Blair Witch Project* overshadowed these historical witchcraft events, and Maryland's Blair Witch became one of the newest eerie characters added to the pages of American folklore.

This particular wicked witch is said to have lived in the forests outside of the small town of Burkittsville in Frederick County. As the story goes, in the 1780s, peasant Elly Kedward of the village of Blair was accused of being an evil witch who had killed several of the town's children. She was banished from the town, tied to a tree in the middle of winter, and left to die. Exactly one year later, all of her accusers and the town's children disappeared. Apparently, she came back and took her revenge. As a result, the remaining people left the town and vowed never to speak the witch's name.

However, in the 1820s, the town of Burkittsville, named after major landowner Henry Burkitt, was founded on the site of the original town of Blair. Unfortunately, the original curse attached itself to the new settlement. Soon unexplained events, murders, missing children, mutilated farm animals, and eerie happenings occurred.

In 1994, the disappearance in the woods of three college film-makers—and the resulting movie—solidified the old legend, delivered it to an international audience, and turned the sleepy village of Burkittsville, Maryland, into a major tourist attraction. The town immediately became a must-see destination for those seeking an up-close-and-personal experience with the mysterious Blair Witch.

There is one problem: The story is total fiction, developed by creative filmmakers who made millions of dollars on the fabricated tale. Their story remains a fine example of regional "fakelore" and a significant illustration of the power of blatant commercialization, proving that there is a powerful public desire to believe that witches live in the woods and things still go bump in the night—and, most importantly, that horror continues to translate into big box office receipts.

But for those seeking the real thing, Carlson's work offers examples of witchcraft trials, accusations, and executions in the Free State. The details, although sometimes sketchy, are there for those willing to seek out official documents and court records.

In 1654, Mrs. Richard Manship was accused of witchcraft. She was not convicted, however, and her accuser Peter Godson was judged to have defamed and slandered her.

In 1654, Mary Lee was hanged at sea as a witch by the crew of the vessel *Charity*.

In 1658, the crew of the ship *Sarah Artch* hanged Elizabeth Richardson at sea as a witch.

In 1661, Joan Mitchell in Charles County was accused of witchcraft and brought suit against four people for slandering her.

In 1665, Elizabeth Bennett of St. Mary's County was accused of witchcraft and acquitted.

In 1674, John Cowman of St. Mary's County was convicted of witchcraft, conjuration, sorcery, or enchantment on the body of Elizabeth Goodale, but he received a reprieve from execution.

In 1685, Rebecca Fowler of Calvert County was executed for witchcraft.

In 1686, Hannah Edwards of Calvert County was acquitted of witchcraft.

In 1702, Katherine Prout of Charles County was charged as being a witch and fined one hundred pounds of tobacco.

In 1712, Virtue Violl of Talbot County, a spinster, was acquitted of the charge of witchcraft.

Certainly the belief in witchcraft arrived with the settlers, traveled the length of the continent with the westward expansion, and even today remains a strong part of America's folklore. Without question, there are many who still believe—or want to believe—in the existence of women in black capes who ride at night on broomsticks and who live in wooded areas and possess magical powers—especially in late October.

Ghost Tours and Resources

The Baltimore Society for Paranormal Research
www.bsprnet.com

Cambridge Historic Ghost Walk
www.dorchesterartscenter.org/ghost.htm

Candlelight Ghost Tours of Frederick
www.marylandghosttours.com

Carroll County Ghost Walk
www.library.carr.org/default.asp

Davidge Hall, University of Maryland Medical College
www.medschool.umaryland.edu/davidge.asp

Fells Point Ghost Tours
www.fellspointghost.com/index.html

Fells Point Ghost Walk
www.baltimore.org/visitors/v_wt_fells_ghost.html

Ghost Tours in Savage Mill
www.marylandghosttours.com/

Ghost Tours of Ellicott City, in Howard County
www.visithowardcounty.com/ghost_tours/index.html

Ghosts of Annapolis Tours
www.ghostsofannapolis.com/

Ghosts of the Prairie
www.prairieghosts.com/

Green Mount Cemetery Tours
Wayne Schaumburg
wschaumburg@earthlink.net

Historic Elk Landing
www.elklanding.org

Historical Society of Cecil County
www.cchistory.org

Maryland Ghost and Spirit Association
www.marylandghosts.com/

The Maryland Paranormal Investigators Coalition
www.marylandparanormal.com

Montgomery County Historical Society
www.montgomeryhistory.org

Mount Harmon Plantation
www.mountharmon.org

Mysterious Maryland Tour Company
www.mysteriousmd.com

Paranormal Research Society of North America
www.paranormalinvestigators.com

Patapsco Female Institute Ghost Tours and Events
www.ellicottcity.net/tourism/attractions/patapsco_female
  _institute

Westminster Ghost Walk
www.carrollcountytourism.org/todo/walking.htm

Bibliography

Books

Anderson, Elizabeth B. *Annapolis: A Walk Through History*. Centreville, MD: Tidewater Publishers, 1984.

Brugger, Robert J. *Maryland: A Middle Temperament, 1634–1980*. Baltimore, MD: The Johns Hopkins University Press, 1988.

Byron, Gilbert. *St. Michaels: The Town That Fooled the British*. St. Michaels, MD: St. Mary's Square Museum, Inc., 1985.

Clark, Jerome. *Unexplained: 347 Strange Sightings, Incredible Occurrences, and Puzzling Physical Phenomena*. Detroit, MI: Visible Ink Press, 1993.

Flowers, Thomas A. *Shore Folklore: Growing Up with Ghosts 'N Legends, Tales, 'N Home Remedies*. Easton, MD: Economy Printing Co., 1989.

Ghost Towns of the Upper Potomac. Oakland, MD: Garrett County Historical Society, 1998.

Hauck, Dennis William. *The National Directory of Haunted Places*. New York: Penguin Books, 1996.

Johnston, George. *History of Cecil County, Maryland*. Baltimore, MD: Genealogical Publishing Co., Inc., 1989.

Legends of St. Mary's: A Collection of Haunts, Witches and Other Strange Occurrences. St. Mary's City, MD: St. Mary's County Historical Society.

Okonowicz, Ed. *Baltimore Ghosts: History, Mystery, Legends and Lore*. Elkton, MD: Myst and Lace Publishers, Inc., 2004.

———. *In the Vestibule*. Elkton, MD: Myst and Lace Publishers, Inc., 1996.

———. *Opening the Door*. Elkton, MD: Myst and Lace Publishers, Inc., 1995.

———. *Phantom in the Bedchamber*. Elkton, MD: Myst and Lace Publishers, Inc., 2000.

———. *Possessed Possessions 2: More Haunted Antiques, Furniture and Collectibles.* Elkton, MD: Myst and Lace Publishers, Inc., 1998.

———. *Terrifying Tales 2 of the Beaches and Bays.* Elkton, MD: Myst and Lace Publishers, Inc., 2002.

———. *Welcome Inn.* Elkton, MD; Myst and Lace Publishers, Inc., 1995.

Okonowicz, Ed, and Jerry Rhodes. *Friends, Neighbors and Folks Down the Road.* Elkton, MD: Myst and Lace Publishers, Inc., 2003.

Papenfuse, Edward C., Gregory A Stiversotn, Susan A. Collins, and Lois Green Carr, eds. *Maryland: A New Guide to the Old Line State.* Baltimore, MD: The Johns Hopkins University Press, 1976.

Roth, Hal. *Now This Is the Truth . . . and Other Lies.* Vienna, MD: Nanticoke Books, 2005.

———. *You Still Can't Get to Puckum, More Folks and Tales from Delmarva.* Vienna, MD: Nanticoke Books, 2000.

Stafford, Moses. *Diary of Yeoman Moses Safford, USS Constellation, 1862–1865.*

Taylor, Troy. *The Haunting of America: Ghosts and Legends from America's Past.* Alton, IL: Whitechapel Productions, 2001.

Trapani, Bob Jr. *Lighthouses of Maryland and Virginia: History, Mystery, Legends and Lore.* Elkton, MD: Myst and Lace Publishers, Inc., 2006.

Articles

Alvarez, Rafael. "Oh, Say, Can You See Ghosts at Fort?" *Baltimore Sun* (October 31, 1996).

———. "Anniversary of Return of Jones' Remains Marked," *The Daily Banner* (July 9, 2005).

Bragdon, Julie. "The Unseen Presence: Ghosts in Annapolis." *Annapolis Magazine* (October 1984).

Burton, Bill. " 'Creature' Is Said To Rise from Bay," *Evening Sun* (September 17, 1980).

Carman, James. "Ghost Stories." *National Parks* (September/October 1986).

Challmes, Joseph J., and Tom Horton. "Marylanders Compile Rich Legacy of Ghostly Tales and Legendary Lore." *Baltimore Sun* (October 31, 1972).

Conboy, Don, and Marian Conboy. "Baltimore's Spookiest Ghost Stories." *Baltimore Magazine* (October 1979).

Doane, William Jr. "Federal Hill." *Baltimore Sun* (November 10, 1999).

"Fear in the Night, Phantom Prowler Terrorizes O'Donnell Heights Residents." *Baltimore Sun* (July 25, 1951).

"Ghostly 'Blue Dog' Still Wags Legend. *Baltimore American* (September 9, 1962).

Lister, Lisa. "Jumpin Catfish . . . It's Chessie Again!" *Kent Island Bay Times* (August 8, 1984).

Martin, Katie. "Tour Stakes out Spots with Spooky Legends." *Baltimore Sun* (October 30, 2005).

"Maryland Superstitions: Sign of a Crowing Hen—Bad Luck To Move Parsley." *Baltimore Sun* (May 1898).

"Marylanders Compile Rich Legacy of Ghostly Tales and Legendary Lore." *Baltimore Sun* (October 31, 1972).

Montgomery, David. "On the Hunt for Haunts." *Washington Post* (October 28, 1993).

Rasmussen, Frederick N. "Emmitsburg's Musical Ghost." *Baltimore Sun* (October 27, 2001).

———. "The Ghostly Light That Spooked Hebron." *Baltimore Sun* (October 29, 2005).

Robinson, Russ. "Elusive 'Chessie' Stumps Computer." *Baltimore Sun* (August 5, 1984).

Sherwood, John. "A Neighborhood Legend, When the Phantom Roamed." *Evening Sun* (February 28, 1962).

Sherwood, John. "Story of Headless Ghost of Peddler's Run Persists." *Baltimore Sun* (July 20, 1960).

Simmons, Melody. "Alleged Ghost Spooks Workers at Courthouse." *Evening Sun* (October 31, 1980).

Starr, John T. "The Ghost of Peddler's Run." *Baltimore Sun* (December 20, 1954).

"U.S. Navy Prepares To Bomb Lone Ghost of Sharps Island." *Baltimore Sun* (May 10, 1938).

Weeks, Linton. "Be True to Your Ghoul." *Washington Post* (October 30, 2002).

White, Michael. "Haunted Neighborhood?" *Cecil Whig* (May 22, 2002).

Online Sources
(in alphabetical order)

Blue Dog Ghost, retrieved September 16, 2006
www.visitcharlescounty.com/cities2.htm

Braddock Treasure, retrieved December 1, 2006
www.post-gazette.com/pg/05167/522060.stm
www.hmdb.org/results.asp?SearchFor = Braddock

Chessie, retrieved September 2006
www.chesapeakebay.net/about.htm
www.unmuseum.org/seasnake.htm
www.s8int.com/dino7.html
www.theshadowlands.net/serpent.htm#ill
www.dnr.state.MDus/irc/chessie/history.html

Dr. Samuel Mudd, retrieved October 18, 2006
www.members.aol.com/RVSNorton/Lincoln29.html
www.www.phrases.org.uk/bulletin_board/5/messages/17.html

Ellicott City Ghosts, retrieved September 22, 2006
www.ellicottcity.net/tourism/attractions/patapsco_female_
    institute/

Emmitsburg Fiddler, retrieved September 22, 2006
www.emmitsburg.net/archive_list/articles/history/stories/
    chrismas_legends.htm

Federal Hill Tunnels, retrieved 2004
www.federalhillonline.com
www.marylandghosts.com/phpbb/viewtopic.php?t = 163

Fells Point, retrieved March 2006
www.columbia.edu/als209/assign2/shipbuilding.html
www.baltimorestories.com/_fp/fp_rd_ghost.html
www.marylandghosts.com/locations/baltimorecity.shtml
www.livebaltimore.com/history/fellspnt.html
www.preservationsociety.com/fellspointwalkngtours2003.html

Fort McHenry National Monument and Historic Shrine,
    retrieved 2004
www.bcpl.net/ ~ etowner/patriot.html

Furnace Creek Slave, retrieved September 30, 2006
www.heritage.uMDedu/CHRSWeb/AssociatedProjects/
    chidesterreport/Chapter%20VI.htm

Goatman, retrieved September 20, 2006
www.atsdr.cdc.gov/HAC/PHA/beltsville/bel_p1.html
www.rundc.com/Doc/MD/PG/BARC.htm

Bibliography

Gold in Montgomery County, retrieved December 2, 2006
www.mgs.md.gov/esic/brochures/gold.html

Hebron Lights, retrieved August 13, 2006
www.astronomycafe.net/weird/lights/hebron3.htm

Jericho Bridge, retrieved February 2006
www.dnr.state.MDus/publiclands/jerusalemhistory.html
jerusalemmill.org/bridge.html

John Paul Jones, retrieved January 2006
www.seacoastnh.com/jpj/burial.html

Phantom Black Dogs, The Folklore of the British Isles, retrieved
    September 18, 2006
www.mysteriousbritin.co.uk/folklore/black_dogs.html

Point Lookout Lighthouse, retrieved February 2006
www.ptlookoutlighthouse.com

Spook Hill, retrieved September 30, 2006
www.dnr.state.MDus/publiclands/spookyparks.html
www.roadsideamerica.com/tips/getAttraction.php3?tip_
    AttractionNo = = 600,

Thomas Dance, retrieved December 1, 2006
www.bayweekly.com/year01/issue9_43/lead9_43.html

USS *Constellation*
www.constellation.org

Wise's Well, retrieved October 9, 2006
www.cmhl.org/fox.html
www.cmhl.org/wise.html

Witches in North America, retrieved September 20, 2006
www.personal.utulsa.edu/ ~ marc-carlson/witchtrial/na.html

Acknowledgments

I WOULD LIKE TO THANK TO KYLE WEAVER OF STACKPOLE BOOKS FOR inviting me to write this book and for giving me the opportunity to learn more about the fascinating state of Maryland. I also appreciate the hard work of production editor Amy Cooper, copyeditor Linda Dalton, and illustrator Heather Adel Wiggins.

Others who assisted in offering material, personal interviews, or information for this book include friends and authors, and colleagues: Hal Roth of Nanticoke Books; Troy Taylor of Whitechapel Press; Bob Trapani, executive director of the American Lighthouse Foundation; and Mike Dixon of the Historical Society of Cecil County.

I also want to acknowledge those folks who provided valuable information and help: Mark N. Schatz of the Ann Arrundell County Historical Society; Mike Hillman of the Emmitsburg Area Historical Society and staff in the Maryland Room in Baltimore's Enoch Pratt Library; Laura Berg and Robert Hall, co-founders of the Point Lookout Lighthouse Preservation Society, for providing a tour of the lighthouse; David Hill and his family for making the arrangements and their hospitality.

For allowing me to use their material from interviews conducted for my book *Baltimore Ghosts: History, Mystery, Legends and Lore,* I want to thank Vince Vaise, park ranger at Fort McHenry National Monument and Historic Shrine; Larry Pitrof, executive director of the Medical Alumni Association of the University of Maryland; and Wayne Schaumburg, cemetery historian and guide at Green Mount Cemetery.

Finally, if I have neglected to mention anyone with whom I had contact during this project, I truly apologize.

About the Author

ED OKONOWICZ IS A STORYTELLER AND A REGIONAL AUTHOR OF MORE than twenty books on Mid-Atlantic culture, oral history, folklore, and ghost stories. As a part-time instructor, he teaches journalism, folklore, and storytelling at the University of Delaware. His books include short story collections, sports biographies, oral history collections, and novels. In 2005 he was voted Best Local Author in the *Delaware Today* magazine readers' poll. One of his books, *Possessed Possessions: Haunted Antiques, Furniture and Collectibles,* led him to appear in October 2005 with psychic James Van Praagh and other paranormal investigators on the Learning Channel two-hour special *Possessed Possessions,* filmed on the *Queen Mary.* His book *Civil War Ghosts at Fort Delaware* is based on ghost/history tours that he has conducted since they began in 1997 at the island prison. His website at www.mystandlace.com provides information on his books and programs.

Other Titles in the
Haunted Series

HAUNTED CONNECTICUT
by Cheri Revai • 0-8117-3296-7

HAUNTED DELAWARE
by Patricia A. Martinelli • 0-8117-3297-5

HAUNTED JERSEY SHORE
by Charles A. Stansfield Jr.
0-8117-3267-3

HAUNTED MAINE
by Charles A. Stansfield Jr. • 0-8117-3373-4

HAUNTED MASSACHUSETTS
by Cheri Revai • 0-8117-3221-5

HAUNTED NEW JERSEY
by Charles A. Stansfield Jr.
and Patricia A. Martinelli
0-8117-3156-1

HAUNTED NEW YORK
by Cheri Revai • 0-8117-3249-5

HAUNTED PENNSYLVANIA
by Mark Nesbitt and Patty A. Wilson
0-8117-3298-3

HAUNTED VERMONT
by Charles A. Stansfield Jr.
0-8117-3399-8

HAUNTED WEST VIRGINIA
by Patty A. Wilson • 0-8117-3400-5

$9.95 each
1-800-732-3669
WWW.STACKPOLEBOOKS.COM